Physical Characteristics of the Griffon Bruxel

(from The Kennel Club bre

C000147882

Body: Short back, level from withers to tail root, neither roaching nor dipping; deep; well-sprung ribs; short, strong loin.

Tail: Customarily docked short.

Hindquarters: Well muscled thighs of good length, hocks low to ground, turning neither in nor out, stifles well bent.

Colour: Clear red, black or black and rich tan without white markings. In clear red, a darker shade on mask and ears desirable. Ideally each hair should be an even red from tip to root.

Size: From 2.2–4.9 kgs (5–11 lbs); most desirable 2.7–4.5 kgs (6–10 lbs).

Feet: Small, thick, cat-like with black toenails.

Griffon Bruxellois

By Juliette Cunliffe

Contents

History of the Griffon Bruxellois 9

Hail a taxi and meet Brussels's nearly-human Griffon! Discover the history of the *'Stable E'curie,'* never a more charming street urchin has captured the hearts of Europeans. Meet the instrumental breeders whose devotion and admiration of the breed have yielded such a unique Toy breed.

Characteristics of the Griffon Bruxellois 24

Come face to 'monkey face' with the Griffon Bruxellois and find out what makes the breed so irresistible, including its physical characteristics and confident, outgoing personality. Owners also learn about the health considerations particular to the breed.

Breed Standard for the Griffon Bruxellois 35

Learn the requirements of a well-bred Griffon Bruxellois by studying the description of the breed as set forth in The Kennel Club's breed standard. Both show dogs and pets must possess key characteristics as outlined in the breed standard.

Your Puppy Griffon Bruxellois 40

Be advised about choosing a reputable breeder and selecting a healthy, typical puppy. Understand the responsibilities of ownership, including home preparation, acclimatisation, the vet and prevention of common puppy problems.

Everyday Care of Your Griffon Bruxellois 66

Enter into a sensible discussion of dietary and feeding considerations, exercise, grooming, travelling and identification of your dog. This chapter discusses Griffon Bruxellois care for all stages of development.

Griffon Bruxellois

Training Your Griffon Bruxellois.................... 88

by Charlotte Schwartz
Be informed about the importance of training your Griffon
Bruxellois from the basics of Housetraining and understanding
the development of a young dog to executing obedience
commands (sit, stay, down, etc.).

Health Care of Your Griffon Bruxellois 113

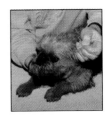

Discover how to select a proper veterinary surgeon and care for
your dog at all stages of life. Topics include vaccination scheduling,
skin problems, dealing with external and internal parasites and the
medical and behavioural conditions common to the breed,
including a special section on canine eye diseases.

Glossary 154

Index 156

All rights reserved.
No part of this book may be reproduced in any
form, by photostat, scanner, microfilm,
xerography or any other means, or incorporated
into any information retrieval system, electronic
or mechanical, without the written permission of
the copyright owner.
Copyright © 2001 Animalia Books, S.L.
Cover patent pending. Printed in Korea.

PUBLISHED IN THE UNITED KINGDOM BY:

INTERPET
P U B L I S H I N G
Vincent Lane, Dorking Surrey RH4 3YX England

ISBN 1-903098-81-5

PHOTO CREDITS:
Norvia Behling, Mary Bloom, TJ Calhoun,
Carolina Biological Supply, Doskocil, Isabelle Français,
James Hayden-Yoav, James R Hayden, RBP,
Carol Ann Johnson, Bill Jonas, C and H G Knebel,
Dwight R Kuhn, Dr Dennis Kunkel, May-He-Co/California,
Mikki Pet Products, Antonio Philippe, Phototake,
Charles Pikulinsky, Dr Robert Pollet, Jean Claude Revy,
Alice Roche, Dr Andrew Spielman, Karen Taylor,
Michael Trafford, Alice van Kempen, Mike and Sue Young.

For over 500 years, dogs of Griffon type have captivated dog lovers. Today's Griffon Bruxellois derives from these unique and charming rough-coated Toy dogs.

History of the

GRIFFON BRUXELLOIS

The history of the Griffon Bruxellois is clearly not a particularly old one in comparison with that of many other breeds, though no one seems to know quite how old it is. Many cynologists have claimed that paintings by Jan van Eyck dating back to 1434 depict the Griffon, but then other doggie scholars claim that the dogs in those pictures are representatives of other breeds.

The breeds involved in the make-up of the Griffon Bruxellois we know today, again, vary according to the source. Count Henry Bylandt considered the breed to be the result of a ruby King Charles Spaniel (also known as the English Toy Spaniel) crossed with an Affenpinscher. Others are convinced that the blood of the Yorkshire Terrier as well as the Irish Terrier flows in the veins of the Griffon Bruxellois. As we shall discover later, the Pug also made its mark on this enchanting breed.

Mrs Parker Rhodes, of Partridge Hill Kennels, was an early and successful exponent of the breed, and in her opinion the breed existed on the Continent from the 16th century, although there was no firm evidence of the Griffon being introduced to England until 1885.

However, we do know that the dog Tom (also sometimes recorded as Vom), who had won at the Brussels Show in 1880, was bought by an Englishman and brought to Britain. Before leaving Belgium, Tom was used at stud and

Four Griffons from the 1930s, rendered by the great dog painter Maud Earl, from left to right, these are Park Place Presto, Park Place Pinkie and Ch Park Place Paristan and Esperance, all owned by Miss Hall.

A German Affenpinscher, illustrated in the late 19th century.

The Irish Terrier, one of the founders of the Griffon stock, was Mr S Wilson's Ch Bolton Woods Mixer, who won 2000 prizes at the turn of the 20th century.

produced a dog called Fox. This male was to become a prominent stud, and is the sire of the very first British champion. There is, though, no record of this import in The Kennel Club Stud Books.

EARLY DAYS IN BELGIUM

In Brussels it appears that Griffons, or at least dogs very similar to them, wandered the streets, for

Mr George Jamison's Sport, an Irish Terrier from 1875, a feisty, go-to-ground sort likely behind the early Griffons.

they were the favourites of the city's coachmen. They called them *'Stable E'curie'* and 'little street urchins,' and they were kept in the stables to work as rat catchers. These dogs are reported to have travelled in the coaches, and, because of their cheeky expressions, became popular with the ladies, as well as with the 'cabbies'!

The Club du Griffon Bruxellois was formed in Belgium in 1880, following which a breed standard was compiled. At a dog show, the first breed classes were

held at the Club in 1883. In 1888 Griffon and Schipperke enthusiasts joined together to form a joint club for their two breeds, and in 1892 a Griffon Bruxellois gained its crown, becoming Belgium's first champion in the breed. In the early 20th century Griffons were judged in classes according to weight, up to 3 kgs (6.5 lbs) and 3–4.5 kgs (6.5–10 lbs).

LADY HANDLEY SPICER

Shortly following the turn of the 20th century Mrs H Handley

This Griffon appeared in the 1930s with Mme Landing of France. The original caption which accompanied the photo stated, 'These dogs need plucking to give them the coat and appearance so much desired. They were first introduced into England about 1894. This dog is said to be the most extravagant dog in the world.'

In the late 1920s, Griffons were popularised by many of England's most prominent families. This photograph of Mrs Parker Rhodes, from 1928, shows the lady with her most attractive Griffons.

Spicer, later to become Lady Handley Spicer of the well-known Copthorne affix, wrote extensively on the breed. She talked of the miners in Yorkshire and the Midlands who owned 'wiry-coated and wiry-dispositioned red dogs.' These dogs accompanied their masters to work and, stowed away in their overcoat pockets until the 'dinner' hour, when they were brought out to share their masters' meals, with an opportunity to catch the occasional rat between times! Lady Handley Spicer said that elderly gentlemen of her day remembered well these little 'red terriers,' saying that they were the originals of the Brussels Griffons (Griffons Bruxellois) of her day. The breed's characteristic gameness was attributed to the sporting activities of the miners. In her opinion, one seldom saw any

Lady Handley Spicer taking her Griffons for a morning walk. Circa 1900.

Pugs were very influential in the development of the smooth Griffons.

pictures from the 19th century bearing much resemblance to the breed as she knew it. The possible exception was the little dog in Sir Edwin Landseer's *Dignity and Impudence*, but she thought it might with equal justice have been claimed as 'a bad Yorkshire or a mongrel Skye Terrier.'

Lady Handley Spicer was a highly respected authority on the breed throughout her life. She died in 1963, at 91 years of age.

THE NAVVY'S DOG

There is an interesting story about a type of dog in Yorkshire known as the 'Navvy's dog,' presumed to be a forerunner of the Yorkshire

This painting by Frances C Fairman shows the four colour varieties of the King Charles Spaniels, as seen in the 1920s. The ruby (solid red) spaniel used in the Griffon's creation is credited for the breed's short face.

Terrier. Around 1873 this dog was sent by a Yorkshire dealer to Belgium. So great was the demand in Belgium that the dealer collected every similar dog he could find and sent them away. Later, in 1898, when interest in the imported Griffons had developed in Britain, this same dog dealer saw them and was convinced that they were nothing more or less than the 'Navvy's dog,' the offspring of the very dogs he had exported!

The tiny Yorkshire Terrier, the world's most popular toy terrier, was likely used in the development of the Griffon.

THE FIRST IMPORTS TO BRITAIN
Griffons Bruxellois were first imported to Britain from Belgium. Here this interesting little breed

This charming photo appeared in 1927 and shows the Hon. Mrs Ionides's Griffons in three sizes, then called 'normal, small and very small.' Breeders were trying to maintain the breed at the smallest size without spoiling the dog's temperament.

'A LADY'S LITTLE DOG'
In the breed standard drawn up by the
original breed club, the opening
section, under the title 'General
Appearance,' reads 'A lady's little dog—
intelligent, sprightly, robust, of
compact appearance—reminding one
of a cob, and captivating the attention
by a quasi-human expression.'

them stand erect, though, of
course, this is no longer allowed
in Britain.

The first known importers to
Britain were Mrs Kingscote, Miss
Adela Gordon, Mrs Frank Pearce
and Fletcher, who kept a dog-
shop in London's Regent Street.
Lady Handley Spicer soon joined
these other enthusiasts and it was
at her house, in 1896, that the
Griffon Bruxellois Club was first
proposed, and later formed. The
Griffon Bruxellois Club of London
was later to become an offshoot of
that club and, as Lady Handley
Spicer put it, like many children,
appeared to be more vigorous
than its parent.

Two years later, in 1898, the
breed was given official recognition by The Kennel Club, with
separate register status, and the
first show at which they were
judged separately from other
breeds was the Ladies Kennel
Association Show that same year.
There were, though, only three
Griffons Bruxellois registered with
The Kennel Club in 1898, two of
which were to become the first

became immediately popular in
the homes of the well-to-do, its
bright and precocious appearance
attracting a number of admirers.
At that time the coat colour was a
paler red than is known today,
and noses were somewhat longer.
Ears were then cropped, to make

UPSTAGED BY A GRIFFON
American movie star Jack Nicholson
shared the screen with a Griffon in the
highly successful *As Good as It Gets*.
This Hollywood film marked the debut
of a Griffon in a starring role and
boasted the breed's popularity in the
USA and abroad.

British champions, Bruno and
Mousequetaire Rouge.

GRIFFONS AT EARLY SHOWS
Griffons made a good impression
when they were first shown at
Crufts Dog Show in February
1895. In the summer of that year,
at the Ranelagh Show a Griffon
weighing 2.25 lbs was shown. She
was called Princess Helene and
had a shorter face than those
previously seen; her eyes were
round, but she did not have the
'monkey-face' that was later
considered so attractive.

Despite the breed's many
admirers, progress up the ladder
of popularity was not so swift as
might have been expected. This
was probably due in part to the

GENUS *CANIS*
Dogs and wolves are
members of the
genus *Canis.*
Wolves are
known
scientifically as
Canis lupus
while dogs are
known as *Canis
domesticus.* Dogs
and wolves are known
to interbreed. The term
canine derives from the Latin
derived word *Canis.* The term
'dog' has no scientific basis but
has been used for thousands of
years. The origin of the word
'dog' has never been
authoritatively ascertained.

The great
Griffon Ch
Copthorne
Talk o' the
Town, painted
by Vernon
Stokes,
published
in 1907.

Published circa 1929, this photo shows a prize winner with cropped ears from the des Nutons kennel in the UK.

fact that the breed was not uniform in type, and that often the name 'Brussels Griffon' was given to a 'mongrel Yorkshire Terrier,' cast some doubt on whether or not people had actually purchased the true Belgian breed.

Breeders worked toward uniformity of type within the breed, and it was the British opinion that by the early 1900s the standard quality of Griffons

A NEW BRITISH CROP

Griffons were originally shown with cropped ears, but in Britain, in 1895, a ruling was brought in that crop-eared dogs could not be shown. This was one of the reasons why early British enthusiasts began to breed their own Griffons, rather than import dogs from Belgium.

Bruxellois on these shores was much higher than in the breed's native land. The breed had become one that possessed an ever-changing expression and, above all, the special characteristic of wonderful eyes, which compared with the eyes of many other toy breeds, appeared as a glass bead to a fathomless lake.

The Alexandra Palace Show was held in September 1900 and it was here that Copthorne Pasha and his son, Ch Copthorne Top-o'-the-Tree, made their first appearance. Pasha was destined to have a great influence on the breed, especially by way of underjaw and true type. For a while, large numbers of prize winners at the principal shows were sired by him. Dogs bearing the Rouge affix were also prominent sires of that era. However, winners still varied

The Griffon Bruxellois is exhibited at shows around the world today. This handsome show dog has successfully competed in shows on the Continent.

The Petit Brabançon, or smooth Griffon, is an handsome dog who proudly grimaces his 'clean-shaven' monkey face.

greatly in size, from under 3 to over 9 lbs (under 1.4 to over 4 kgs).

THE MONKEY FACE

Clever breeding of Continental fanciers brought about the monkey-like expression, a feature of today's breed standard for the Griffon Bruxellois. On the Continent, the Pug Dog and ruby King Charles Spaniel were incorporated into breeding programmes, and it was these introductions that are thought responsible for the short face and large eyes, as well as for the breed's large nostrils and brilliantly coloured coat.

PETIT BRABANÇONS

The Pug was also responsible for introducing a smooth-coated variety of the breed, which is produced in the same litter as the rough coat. This was earlier called the Brabançon Griffon, but later

WHIN WINS
Belgium's Queen Mary was keenly interested in the Griffon and upon her death, her dog, Whin, was left to the care of a servant. Whin received a legacy equal to £2000, so that the dog might enjoy all it needed for the remainder of its life.

became known in Europe as the Petit Brabançon. Before World War I, Challenge Certificates were available in Britain both for rough and for smooth Griffons, indicating recognition of the two varieties of coat within the breed even then. Now in Britain, smooths are shown alongside the rough-coated members of the breed and all are simply called Griffon Bruxellois.

According to Lady Handley Spicer, the period of 12 years or so prior to 1907 saw a certain advance in the evolution of the

A group of Griffons with cropped ears, photographed in Belgium, circa 1907.

EAR CROPPING

Ear cropping consists of the ear leather being surgically trimmed and the ear is trained to stand upright. Originally cropping was to prevent the ears from being bitten by any adversary. With the fighting dogs, and terriers, it gave the opponent less to hang on to. Ear cropping was considered important for cosmetic purposes as it gives the dog a very smart look. Fortunately, today the barbaric tradition of cropping ears has been banned in the UK, and dogs with cropped ears cannot be shown. Dogs can be shown in the United States with either cropped or uncropped ears but they are rarely seen in the ring with uncropped ears. American breeders still prefer cropped ears since their breeding programmes have essentially ignored ear type for generations.

Griffon. When the breed first arrived in Britain, the underjaw was considered of little or no importance, but in those first few years it had come to be recognised as one of the most important physical features of the breed. Red pin-wire coats were also rarely seen in the breed's formative years in Britain, but in time these coats became much desired. However, within one litter, Griffon puppies varied considerably in type, size and colouring, more than with most other breeds.

THE WAR YEARS

Despite the difficulties in Belgium during World War I, people managed to continue a little breeding and were able to export the breed again. However, in Belgium, some decline came about between the wars because it was decided not to breed from any web-footed dogs, causing numbers to decline dramatically. (Web feet, incidentally, still turn up in Griffon litters from time to time.) During World War II, there was no breeding at all, so that the Griffon Bruxellois very nearly disappeared in its homeland until British stock was re-introduced there.

Despite its endearing looks and personality, the Griffon Bruxellois has never been an especially numerically strong breed in Britain. Although there was a rise in numbers during the 1950s, peaking in 1962 to a high of 627 in terms of Kennel Club

A GRIFFON TO DYE FOR!

In the early days of the Griffon's introduction to Britain, breeders profited highly from their sales. Those weighing under 6 lbs (2.8 kgs) and of rich colour were the most highly sought after. Occasionally, unscrupulous dealers resorted to dyeing the dogs to obtain the highest prices!

A black smooth Griffon shows his identical physical structures to the rough Griffon sans the wire coat and furnishings.

THE GREAT RAT SWAP

An amazing story about a dealer faking a Griffon comes from the outskirts of Paris where a Griffon was doing tricks, much to the delight of onlookers. A prospective lady purchaser was persuaded to buy an even smaller Griffon, kept in the man's pocket. Upon arriving home with her new acquisition, it bolted up the curtain rail, and when retrieved, to the new owner's horror, the little 'dog' was revealed to be a rat, sewn up in a Griffon's skin.

registration figures, there has since been a steady decline. In recent years there have only been around 200 new registrations per annum, similar to the numbers registered in the 1920s and 1930s.

THE GRIFFON IN THE ANTIPODES

A Griffon was first exported to Australia in 1909, but the breed was little known until 1936 when appearing at the Royal Melbourne Show, under an English judge. The first Griffon club in that country, however, was not set up until 1975. In New Zealand, Griffons did not arrive until 1945, but in both countries the breed has a dedicated band of followers.

A black rough Griffon with the endearing facial expression that attracts so many admirers to the breed.

BRAIN AND BRAWN

Since dogs have been inbred for centuries, their physical and mental characteristics are constantly being changed to suit man's desires for hunting, retrieving, scenting, guarding and warming their masters' laps. During the past 150 years, dogs have been judged according to physical characteristics as well as functional abilities. Few breeds can boast a genuine balance between physique, working ability and temperament.

Among the most celebrated of modern Griffons is Ch Marquant Miss Scarlet. This English bitch is considered to be very close to the modern breed standard.

GRIFFONS IN SWEDEN

It was around 1910 that the breed first appeared in Sweden, their bloodlines primarily being Belgian. Not until the 1930s did the breed gain popularity, when English imports made their mark both in the show ring and in breeding programmes. Unfortunately, the ban on tail docking has hit the breed hard in Sweden, and several breeders having abandoned their breeding programmes entirely. This will undoubtedly be to the future detriment of the breed.

THE NETHERLANDS

In the Netherlands, the Dutch Smoushond, a breed sharing the same roots as the Griffon Bruxellois, existed at much the same time. '*Smous*' is actually the Dutch word for '*griffon.*' However, in the Netherlands the breed remained as it had always been, a tough little working dog that looked more like a mongrel! The first Griffons were registered in the country in 1897, and a club was formed in 1919. Since then there have always been a small number of the breed in the Netherlands, but regrettably no lines have survived to the present day.

THE BRUSSELS GRIFFON IN AMERICA

It was in 1899 that the first Griffon gained entry into the American Kennel Club's Stud Book, since which time the breed has had a steady following, albeit small in number. The official breed name in America is, indeed, Brussels Griffon. By the 1980s, several representatives had achieved high awards in the show rings, with Group and Best in Show wins among them. In 1988, the top-winning Toy dog in the country was none other than a Brussels Griffon!

THE GRIFFON IN ART

The earliest picture with which the Griffon breed is connected is *The Marriage of Arnolfini and Giovanna Cenani*, painted by Jan van Eyck in 1434. However, it must be appreciated that other breeds also lay claim to the dog in this picture, so it is likely that this dog is, in fact, a forerunner of more than one single breed.

Detail from the painting *The Marriage of Arnolfini and Giovanna Cenani*, Jan van Eyck, 1434.

In the 16th century, Jacope de Empolin was another who depicted dogs of this general type in his work, while in 1870 Renoir painted *La Baigneuse au Griffon*. This understandably leads people to think that this surely must have been the Griffon breed we know today (which indeed it may have been), but it should also be appreciated that the word '*griffon*' simply means 'rough-coated' and many breeds fit that description. Also connected with the breed is a painting in 1883 by Barbu, entitled *Le Chien*.

Characteristics of the
GRIFFON BRUXELLOIS

WHY THE GRIFFON BRUXELLOIS?

Those who choose to live with a Griffon Bruxellois probably do so because this is a breed that possesses a unique combination of impudence coupled with dignity and intelligence, not to mention an impish sense of humour! Many say that this is a big dog in a small package, and that probably sums up the Griffon well.

Many will recall the late Stanley Dangerfield, presenter of the Crufts television programme among others, well-known judge and an owner of Griffons. In 1971 he wrote that this was a controversial breed, and that no two people saw it alike. 'Some,' he said, 'consider it wholly beautiful, others extremely ugly. Indeed the one point upon which there is complete agreement is that it is quaint, unusual and full of character.'

The breed is more popular in Britain and the rest of Europe than in the USA, but wherever it lives, this is a loving companion, with many engaging ways; it is only surprising that the breed is not more popular than it is. Having said that, many other breeds that have suddenly multiplied have lost something in the process, so it is to be hoped that this breed's dedicated band of followers will keep the Griffon just as it is, very special and unique.

PERSONALITY

The Griffon has something of the disposition of a terrier, for after all, terrier blood undoubtedly lies somewhere in the breed's ancestral past. Like terriers, the Griffon is lively and alert, always one to command attention.

This breed abounds with confidence and good humour, but is fearless and distinctly determined. A Griffon usually gets on well with other animals and rarely seems afraid to stand up to dogs much larger than himself. For this reason, when mixing with unknown dogs, owners should take care that no harm is likely to occur to the diminutive confident fellow!

In general, the Griffon is a happy, affectionate and adaptable little dog, who always loves his

Although counted among the Toy group, the Griffon Bruxellois is an active and trainable little dog that excels in organised canine activities, such as agility trials.

master or mistress most of all, but can be a touch shy with strangers or in unfamiliar surroundings. It is important to show a Griffon puppy firmly that you are the boss, not he, otherwise he might just develop bad habits. An American's description of her own Griffon as 'the devil incarnate cloaked in a furry suit' perhaps paints a sufficiently vivid picture without elaborating further.

PHYSICAL CHARACTERISTICS
Although the breed is small, it is definitely not one of the more delicate Toy breeds. In shape this is a cobby little dog, giving a well-balanced square outline, with a short back and well-sprung rib cage. The term 'cobby' actually comes from the Welsh cob pony, which, as everyone knows, is a sturdy little animal.

The Griffon should be heavy for its size, indicating that there should be plenty of bone and muscle, albeit in small compass. This is a hardy and compact dog, but should never be coarse.

In comparison with the size of body, the Griffon's head is large, and in rough-coated dogs the hair on the skull is rather coarse, and the hair on muzzle and chin form a beard, giving a distinctive appearance which, once seen, can never be forgotten.

The head is undoubtedly one of the breed's most important features, and the old description of a 'quasi-human expression' is very apt. The skull is not so flat as that of a Pekingese, nor so domed as that of the King Charles Spaniel; it is just slightly

Handily sized, the Griffon can make use of a 'cat door,' giving your dog free access to the garden.

IT'S NEVER TOO LATE...
A Griffon of 14.5 years mated a bitch, even though he was a pet and had never been used at stud. This shows that owners should always take care to keep bitches away from dogs when they are in season— however old the dog! Being a long-lived breed, it is likely that Griffon males even older than this have also mated bitches.

squarely, the lower one protruding just a little, to give that characteristic 'turn-up,' enhanced by the prominence of the chin.

Another physical feature, characteristic of this breed, is the rather wide chest, enabling the straight forelegs to be set some distance apart. The Griffon has well-muscled hindquarters and, when typically constructed, they will allow good driving power from the rear.

The black nose has wide open nostrils, enabling the Griffon to breathe normally.

rounded, and also rounded at the temples, adding to the characteristic expression of the breed. It is very important that the black nose has wide-open nostrils, for this prevents breathing difficulties. When viewed from the front, the top of the nose is level with the centre of the eyes, which are very dark, large, round, clear and alert. The eye rims should be black, though, unfortunately, they are not always so. The muzzle is wide and the neat lips should meet

Size

Although undoubtedly a small dog, there is a fairly wide variation in size, for the breed standard allows weights from 2.2 kgs (5 lbs) to 5 kgs (11 lbs), although weights reasonably well within this range are the most desirable. Even small Griffons should weigh heavy in comparison with their size, but within the breed some taller dogs can weigh less than small ones that possess more substantial bone.

Coat

In Britain, there are two different textures of coat in the Griffon Bruxellois, rough and smooth. The latter is short and tight and should not feel silky to the touch. In some smooths, there is a very dense undercoat, creating both a thick mane and a 'bustle.' In general, smooth-coated Griffons have slightly longer hair on the shoulders.

Rough-coated dogs have a harsh coat, though rarely so wiry as that of the Fox Terrier, for example. There should be no curl, but some Griffons with a particularly wiry coat and an especially dense undercoat tend to have a bit of a wave. An undercoat is admired but is not always present. Rough-coated dogs need to be hand-stripped to maintain the correct coat texture.

While smooth-coated dogs have a seasonal shed, the roughs do not. Instead each hair grows to a length of 3 to 4 inches and then dies as a new hair grows in the

TAKING CARE

Science is showing that as people take care of their pets, the pets are taking care of their owners. A study in 1998, published in the *American Journal of Cardiology,* found that having a pet can prolong his owner's life. Pet owners have lower blood pressure, and pets help their owners to relax and keep them more physically fit. It was also found that pets help to keep the elderly connected to their community.

A Griffon with a smooth coat in a clear red coloration.

follicle. In general, the Griffon Bruxellois is not a suitable pet for those who suffer from allergies, though understandably a good deal will depend on the sensitivity causing the allergy.

Colour

For proper show dogs, colours are clear red, black or black with rich tan; on none of these should there be any white markings. Of course, in pet dogs, colour is quite insignificant and guided by the owner's preferences. The author here describes the colours as guided by the breed standard, information of interest to all Griffon lovers and especially show dog aficionados.

The reds vary from dark mahogany, through a fiery red, to fawn, but provided the coat is red, the actual shade does not matter greatly to breeders or judges.

Having said that, the fawn must have a reddish tinge, for without this the colour is incorrect in the eyes of the judge. In clear reds a darker mask and ears are desirable, though these attributes are more commonly found in smooths than in roughs.

Blacks should be of good solid colour, although younger dogs quite frequently have a rusty hue, or even a silvery undercoat. Blacks, incidentally, tend to grow more hair inside and outside the ear, so when grooming, extra attention is necessary in this area.

Black and tans are now the rarest of the colours found in Griffons. They were more popular in the past, the first of this colour to become a champion gaining its crown in 1930. However, 21 years passed before the second black and tan was made a champion.

Brindle and black-tinged mahogany are incorrect, and in Britain a mixture of black and red hairs is also incorrect. However, the latter is accepted on the

MEET MR DANGERFIELD
Griffon enthusiast and judge, Stanley Dangerfield presented the television programme *The Good Companions* for five years during the 1950s. The programme featured his own little red smooth Griffon, named Tazzie. Another of his dogs, Ch Chosendale Seamus was one of the only black and tan smooth Griffon champions in the history of the breed.

Continent where this is one of the colours incorporated under the breed name, Griffon Belge, as distinct from Griffon Bruxellois and Petit Brabançon.

TEETH

Although neither teeth nor tongue should show, unlike the majority of breeds, the Griffon has a slightly undershot bite, the lower teeth protruding slightly beyond the upper ones, this in keeping with the required facial expression.

EARS

Ears of the Griffon should be semi-erect, standing a little above the level of the skull, and with flaps falling neatly forward to cover the section of the ear that is erect. Ears still vary quite considerably within the breed, but the smaller the ear the better.

BLACK IS BEAUTIFUL
By the 1930s, black Griffons were quite common, the colour having derived from the black Pug. The breed's first black champion was Ch Nofa Gollywog, gaining his title in 1916. Black and tan was by no means rare but was greatly valued, usually occurring when two smooth reds of brilliant colours had been mated together.

The adult bite of a Griffon, showing how the lower teeth protrude slightly to contribute to the breed's facial expression.

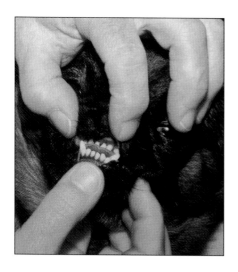

TAILS

Although the subject of tail docking remains a matter for debate in Europe, the tail of the Griffon Bruxellois is customarily docked short. The length of tail varies somewhat from puppy to puppy, so it is difficult to be precise about the amount of tail that is docked. However, it should always be left sufficiently long to create a stop to the length of the level back, at the point where the tail emerges. It is important that the tail is set on high, emerging at a right angle, thereby enabling it to be carried high, which is typical for the breed.

In some countries tail docking is not permitted at all, and tails left at their full length seem currently to vary considerably in their appearance. With the recent relaxation of quarantine laws in Britain, it is highly likely that docked and undocked Griffons will find themselves standing side by side in the judging ring, presenting a difficult exercise for the eye of the judge!

HEALTH CONSIDERATIONS

Although breeding Griffons is not always easy, once a litter has been produced and the puppies have overcome the first few crucial weeks of life, this is, in general, a

World-wide there is considerable variation in the length of the Griffon's tail since tail docking laws vary from country to country. This is a docked tail about the length usual for the Griffon.

DOGS, DOGS, GOOD FOR YOUR HEART!
People usually purchase dogs for companionship, but studies show that dogs can help to improve their owners' health and level of activity, as well as lower a human's risk of coronary heart disease. Without even realising it, when a person puts time into exercising, grooming and feeding a dog, he also puts more time into his own personal health care. Dog owners establish a more routine schedule for their dogs to follow, which can have positive effects on a human's health. Dogs also teach us patience, offer unconditional love and provide the joy of having a furry friend to pet!

healthy breed. They are hardy little dogs, but as with all breeds illness can befall them, so it is always wise to be aware of some of the problems that might possibly occur.

WEB-FOOTED GRIFFONS

Occasionally Griffons have webbed feet. They are not truly webbed, but the two centre toes on the front feet (sometimes on the back feet too) are joined together. In Belgium, breeding from such Griffons was banned, but this has never been the case in Britain, and no problems have been encountered. It may be the result of a throwback to the Pyrame, a now extinct ancestor of the King Charles Spaniel.

OESTRUS

Some Griffon bitches have clear seasons, in which they show no sign of colour while they are on heat. This understandably makes it difficult for an owner to know when a bitch should be kept away from males; and, if a mating is planned, this makes it difficult to work out when the time of mating is likely to be right. A further complication when planning matings, and one of the reasons why it is not easy to breed from Griffons, is that often a bitch is in season only for a very short while.

CLEFT PALATE

Occasionally puppies can be born with cleft palate, so it is essential to check for this as soon as puppies have been whelped. This can be done by opening the puppy's mouth and checking with one's little finger that the ridge-like roof of the mouth is fully present. Should there appear to be any deformity a vet must be consulted immediately, for except in very minor cases, the fairest thing is to have the puppy put to sleep before it suffers any further.

It is always sensible to have both bitch and puppies checked over by a vet soon after birth, so if there is any doubt at all about whether cleft palate is present,

DISASTROUS GARDENERS

Griffons are terrible gardeners, but if only someone could tell them the difference between weeds and flowers they would be of invaluable help to the ardent gardening enthusiast. Without guidance, they especially seem to adore pulling up colourful flowers!

one's vet will be able to ascertain this and deal with it accordingly.

HEAT STROKE

Just occasionally a Griffon can collapse as a result of heat stroke. It is therefore particularly important not to allow Griffons to get too hot, such as they would do if left in a car, even with the windows open on a relatively mild day! Heat stroke is highly

The large eyes of the Griffon are an important characteristic of the breed.

dangerous and a frightening experience, so must be avoided at all costs.

Veterinary assistance should be sought immediately, but initially the dog should be kept quiet and as cool as possible, with very cold water applied to head, neck and shoulders. If the dog has lost consciousness, no attempt must be made to force him to drink, but once consciousness has been regained, offer glucose water or a light saline solution.

It is always a sensible precaution to allow Griffons to travel with a non-spill water bowl in their travelling compartment; this way at least they have access to a drink of water if they begin to feel the heat.

CORRECTIVE SURGERY

Surgery is often used to correct genetic bone diseases in dogs. Usually the problems present themselves early in the dog's life and must be treated before bone growth stops.

EYE PROBLEMS

Because the Griffon's eyes are large, they are more susceptible to damage than the eyes of many other breeds. It is therefore essential for eyes to be kept clear of debris and discharge, which can be helped by keeping the area around the eyes free from hair. Cat owners should also take care that their Griffon's eyes are not damaged by a cat's claws, as this can all too easily cause damage. Should ever there be evidence of a scratch, ulcer or heavier than usual discharge, veterinary advice should be sought without delay. Although by no means are cataracts prevalent in the breed, some owners like to have

SKIN PROBLEMS

Eczema and dermatitis are skin problems that occur in many breeds and they can often be a tricky problem to solve. Frequent bathing of the dog will remove skin oils and will cause the problem to worsen. Allergies to food or something in the environment can also cause the problem. Consider trying homeopathic remedies in addition to seeing your vet for direction.

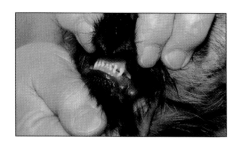

their dogs' eyes tested for signs of early cataract.

UMBILICAL HERNIAS

An umbilical hernia, seen as a small swelling at the sight of the umbilicus, is not uncommon in the breed. Such hernias can be hereditary or, possibly more frequently, be caused by a bitch tugging too forcefully on the umbilical cord. Most hernias are entirely trouble-free, but it is always wise to ask a vet to check the hernia for sometimes surgical rectification is needed.

SNORTING

Some Griffons, like many others of the short-nosed breeds, suffer from snorting, which is caused by elongation of the soft palate. Although frightening for the novice owner, this is rarely a problem. The dog will usually stand four-square with sides heaving, but the problem will go away almost as soon as it came. To help alleviate the situation, it is a good idea to place one's thumb over the dog's nose, causing the dog to breathe

through its mouth, following which breathing will return to normal.

BABY TEETH

Some Griffon puppies have a tendency to retain their baby teeth longer than expected, but breeders' opinions vary as to whether or not these teeth should be removed by a vet, thereby allowing the new ones to grow through in the correct position. Whether or not it is sensible to subject a puppy to a light anaesthetic, which could be avoided, is a matter for debate.

LUXATING PATELLAS

A problem from which some Griffons can suffer is luxating patella, which is trouble with the knee joints and is common to many of the Toy breeds. A sign of

The baby teeth of a Griffon are retained for a longer period of time than in most other breeds.

DO YOU WANT TO LIVE LONGER?
If you like to volunteer, it is wonderful if you can take your dog to a nursing home once a week for several hours. The elder community loves to have a dog to visit with and often your dog will bring a bit of companionship to someone who is lonely or somewhat detached from the world. You will be not only bringing happiness to someone else but keeping your little dog busy—and we haven't even mentioned the fact that they have discovered that volunteering helps to increase your own longevity!

this is the dog's limping or carrying one leg off the ground when running. This is because a bone has slipped out of position, due either to injury or to poor alignment. It is an important factor that a dog so affected is not allowed to become overweight, as this is likely to exacerbate the problem.

Many dogs with luxating patella live with the problem without experiencing pain, but surgery is sometimes required. A veterinary testing procedure is available.

LEGG-CALVE-PERTHES DISEASE

Although unusual in the Griffon, Legg-Calve-Perthes disease is worthy of mention. This is necrosis of the femoral head and is believed to be hereditary, as in general it seems to be noticed more in some family bloodlines. It occurs more in the smaller breeds of dog than in larger ones. Initial lameness slowly becomes worse, eventually causing the dog to carry the affected limb. With time, due to disuse, the muscles of the thigh and upper leg disappear and the head of the femur becomes distorted. This condition can encourage further joint pain and osteoarthritis. Clearly veterinary advice should be sought at the first sign of lameness.

Only radiographic evaluation by an experienced veterinary surgeon can ascertain whether the dog has a luxating patella (kneecap). Compare the x-rays of a normal kneecap (right) and an abnormal one.

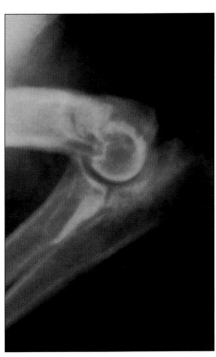

Breed Standard for the
GRIFFON BRUXELLOIS

INTRODUCTION TO
THE BREED STANDARD

The breed standard for the Griffon Bruxellois is set down by The Kennel Club and, like standards for other breeds, can be changed occasionally. Such changes come about usually with guidance from experienced people from within the breed clubs, but it should be understood that in Britain The Kennel Club has the final word as to what is incorporated, and in what manner.

It is interesting to note changes that have come about over the years, such as that the colour grey was included in the standard in use around the turn of the 20th century, though there was no mention of the colour black, just black and tan. The standard then required the eyes to be 'black, or nearly black,' but eventually this description was thought to be misleading, as no dog can have truly black eyes. Today the standard requires them to be 'very dark,' which is much more realistic.

All breed standards are designed effectively to paint a picture in words, though each reader will almost certainly have a slightly different way of interpreting these words. After all, when all is said and done, were everyone to interpret a breed's standard in exactly the same way, there would only be one consistent winner within the breed at any given time!

In any event, to fully comprehend the intricacies of a breed, reading words alone is never enough. In addition, it is essential for devotees to watch the Griffon Bruxellois being judged at shows and, if possible, to attend seminars at which the breed is discussed. This enables owners to absorb as much as possible about this thoroughly charming and unique little breed. 'Hands on' experience, providing an opportunity to assess the structure of dogs, is always valuable, especially for those who hope ultimately to judge the breed.

However familiar one is with the breed, it is always worth refreshing one's memory by re-reading the standard, for it is sometimes all too easy to overlook, or perhaps forget, certain features.

A breed standard undoubtedly helps breeders to produce stock

The Griffon Bruxellois who most closely conforms to the standard will be taking home the ribbons. This smooth Griffon and his proud owner have had a remarkable day on the show scene.

that comes as close as possible to the recognised standard and helps judges to know what they are looking for. This enables judges to make a carefully considered decision when selecting the most typical Griffon Bruxellois to head their line of winners.

THE KENNEL CLUB STANDARD FOR THE GRIFFON BRUXELLOIS

Both the smooth and rough Griffon possess a pert, monkey-like expression.

General Appearance: A cobby, well-balanced, square little dog, giving appearance of measuring the same from withers to tail root as from withers to ground.

Characteristics: Smart little dog with disposition of a terrier. Two varieties, rough coated, Griffon Bruxellois and smooth coated, Petit Brabançon. Both with pert, monkey-like expression, heavy for size.

Temperament: Lively and alert.

Head and Skull: Head large in comparison to body, rounded but in no way domed, wide between the ears. Hair on skull, in roughs rather coarse. Nose always black, as short as possible with large open nostrils, high set sloping back to skull with deep stop between nose and skull. Wide muzzle, neat lips, with good turn-up. Chin prominent, in roughs furnished with beard.

Eyes: Black-rimmed, very dark, large, round, clear and alert.

Ears: Semi-erect, high-set, the smaller the better.

Mouth: Slightly undershot with even teeth, not showing teeth or tongue.

Neck: Medium length, slightly arched, springing from well laid back shoulders.

Forequarters: Chest rather wide and deep, legs straight of medium length and bone.

The Griffon's head should show a deep stop between the nose and skull.

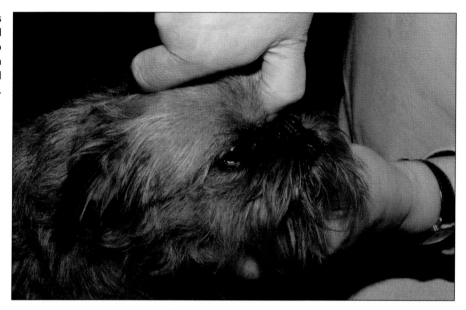

THE IDEAL SPECIMEN

According to The Kennel Club, 'The Breed Standard is the "Blueprint" of the ideal specimen in each breed approved by a governing body, e.g. The Kennel Club, the Fédération Cynologique International (FCI) and the American Kennel Club.

'The Kennel Club writes and revises Breed Standards taking account of the advice of Breed Councils/Clubs. Breed Standards are not changed lightly to avoid "changing the standard to fit the current dogs" and the health and well-being of future dogs is always taken into account when new standards are prepared or existing ones altered.'

Body: Short back, level from withers to tail root, neither roaching nor dipping; deep; well-sprung ribs; short, strong loin.

Hindquarters: Well muscled thighs of good length, hocks low to ground, turning neither in nor out, stifles well bent.

Feet: Small, thick, cat-like with black toenails.

Tail: Customarily docked short, carried high, emerging at right angles from level topline.

Gait/Movement: Free with good drive from rear. Moving true coming and going. High stepping front movement undesirable.

A smooth Griffon exhibiting the black and tan coloration.

Coat: *Roughs:* harsh, wiry, free from curl, preferably with undercoat. *Smooths:* short and tight.

Colour: Clear red, black or black and rich tan without white markings. In clear red, a darker shade on mask and ears desirable. Ideally each hair should be an even red from tip to root. Frosting on muzzles of mature smooths should not be penalised.

Size: From 2.2–4.9 kgs (5–11 lbs); most desirable 2.7–4.5 kgs (6–10 lbs).

Faults: Any departure from the foregoing points should be considered a fault and the seriousness with which the fault should be regarded should be in exact proportion to its degree.

Note: Male animals should have two apparently normal testicles fully descended into the scrotum.

BREEDER'S BLUEPRINT
If you are considering breeding your bitch, it is very important that you are familiar with the breed standard. Reputable breeders breed with the intention of producing dogs that are as close as possible to the standard, and contribute to the advancement of the breed. Study the standard for both physical appearance and temperament, and make certain your bitch and your chosen stud dog measure up.

HOW TO SELECT A PUPPY

Before reaching the decision that you will look for a Griffon Bruxellois puppy, it is essential that you are fully clear in your mind that this is the most suitable breed, both for you and for your family.

You should have done plenty of background 'homework' on the breed, and preferably have visited a few breed club or Championship Shows, giving you an opportunity to see the breed in some numbers. This will have provided you with the opportunity to see the dogs with their breeders and owners, and you will hopefully have had a chance to see not only those with the more familiar rough coat but also smooth-coated ones. These things are important, for you may decide you have a preference where coat, or even colour, is concerned.

Remember that the dog you select should remain with you for the duration of its life, which is usually upwards of 14 years, so making the right decision from the outset is of the utmost importance. No dog should be moved from one home to another,

simply because its owners were not considerate enough to have done sufficient background homework before selecting the breed.

It is unlikely that you will find many litters of Griffon Bruxellois available for sale at any given time, which means you may well have to put your name on a waiting list with the breeder of your choice. However, always remember that when looking for a puppy, a good breeder will be assessing you as a prospective new owner, just as carefully as you are selecting the breeder.

Always be certain that the puppy you finally choose has a sound personality; it should not be shy nor aggressive. Never take pity on an unduly shy puppy, for in doing so you will be asking for trouble in the long term as such a dog is likely to have serious problems in socialising.

Puppies almost invariably look enchanting, but you must select one from a caring breeder who has given the puppies all the attention they have deserved and has looked after them well. They

A lovely Griffon puppy at ten weeks of age, about the age most breeders release pups to new owners. Are you ready for such a tiny but giant responsibility?

should already have been well socialised and this is likely to be apparent when you meet them.

The puppy you select should look well fed, but not pot-bellied, as this might indicate worms. Eyes should look bright and clear, without discharge. The nose should be moist, an indication of good health, but should never be runny. Moreover, there should certainly be no evidence of loose motions nor of parasites. The puppy you choose should also have a healthy-looking coat, an important indicator of good health internally.

PUPPY APPEARANCE
Your puppy should have a well-fed appearance but not a distended abdomen, which may indicate worms or incorrect feeding, or both. The body should be firm, with a solid feel. The skin of the abdomen should be pale pink and clean, without signs of scratching or rash. Check the hind legs to make certain that dewclaws were removed, if any were present at birth.

INSURANCE
Many good breeders will offer you insurance with your new puppy, which is an excellent idea. The first few weeks of insurance will probably be covered free of charge or with only minimal cost, allowing you to take up the policy when this expires. If you own a pet dog, it is sensible to take out such a policy as veterinary fees can be high, although routine vaccinations and boosters are not covered. Look carefully at the many options open to you before deciding which suits you best.

Something else to consider is whether or not to take out veterinary insurance. Vet's bills can mount up, and you must always be certain that sufficient funds are available to give your dog any veterinary attention that may be needed. Keep in mind, though, that routine vaccinations will not be covered.

COMMITMENT OF OWNERSHIP
After considering all of these factors, you have most likely made some very important decisions about selecting your puppy. You have chosen a Griffon, which means that you have decided which characteristics you want in a dog and what type of dog will best fit into your family

and lifestyle. If you have selected a breeder, you have gone a step further—you have done your research and found a responsible, conscientious person who breeds quality Griffons and who should be a reliable source of help as you and your puppy adjust to life together. If you have observed a litter in action, you have obtained a firsthand look at the dynamics

PUPPY SELECTION

Your selection of a good puppy can be determined by your needs. A show potential or a good pet? It is your choice. Every puppy, however, should be of good temperament. Although show-quality puppies are bred and raised with emphasis on physical conformation, responsible breeders strive for equally good temperament. Do not buy from a breeder who concentrates solely on physical beauty at the expense of personality.

DOCUMENTATION

Two important documents you will get from the breeder are the pup's pedigree and registration certificate. The breeder should register the litter and each pup with The Kennel Club, and it is necessary for you to have the paperwork if you plan on showing or breeding in the future.

Make sure you know the breeder's intentions on which type of registration he will obtain for the pup. There are limited registrations which may prohibit the dog from being shown, bred or from competing in non-conformation trials such as Working or Agility if the breeder feels that the pup is not of sufficient quality to do so. There is also a type of registration that will permit the dog in non-conformation competition only.

On the reverse side of the registration certificate, the new owner can find the transfer section which must be signed by the breeder.

of a puppy 'pack' and, thus, you should learn about each pup's individual personality—perhaps you have even found one that particularly appeals to you.

However, even if you have not yet found the Griffon puppy of your dreams, observing pups will help you learn to recognise certain behaviour and to determine what a pup's behaviour indicates about his temperament. You will be able to pick out

DID YOU KNOW?
Breeders rarely release puppies until they are eight to ten weeks of age. This is an acceptable age for most breeds of dog, excepting Toy breeds, which are not released until around 12 weeks, given their petite sizes. If a breeder has a puppy that is 12 weeks or more, it is likely well socialised and housetrained. Be sure that it is otherwise healthy before deciding to take it home.

possible are all important steps on the way to dog ownership. It may seem like a lot of effort...and you have not even taken the pup home yet! Remember, though, you cannot be too careful when it comes to deciding on the type of dog you want and finding out about your prospective pup's background. Buying a puppy is not—or should not be—just another whimsical purchase. This is one instance in which you actually do get to choose your own family! You may be thinking that buying a puppy should be fun—it should not be so serious and so much work. Keep in mind that your puppy is not a cuddly stuffed toy or decorative lawn ornament, but a creature that will become a real member of your family. You will come to realise that, while buying a puppy is a pleasurable and exciting endeavour, it is not something to be taken lightly. Relax...the fun will start when the pup comes home!

Always keep in mind that a puppy is nothing more than a baby in a furry disguise...a baby

which pups are the leaders, which ones are less outgoing, which ones are confident, which ones are shy, playful, friendly, aggressive, etc. Equally as important, you will learn to recognise what a healthy pup should look and act like. All of these things will help you in your search, and when you find the Griffon that was meant for you, you will know it!

Researching your breed, selecting a responsible breeder and observing as many pups as

ARE YOU A FIT OWNER?
If the breeder from whom you are buying a puppy asks you a lot of personal questions, do not be insulted. Such a breeder wants to be sure that you will be a fit provider for his puppy.

PREPARING FOR PUP

Unfortunately, when a puppy is bought by someone who does not take into consideration the time and attention that dog ownership requires, it is the puppy who suffers when he is either abandoned or placed in a shelter by a frustrated owner. So all of the 'homework' you do in preparation for your pup's arrival will benefit you both. The more informed you are, the more you will know what to expect and the better equipped you will be to handle the ups and downs of raising a puppy. Hopefully, everyone in the household is willing to do his part in raising and caring for the pup. The anticipation of owning a dog often brings a lot of promises from excited family members: 'I will walk him every day,' 'I will feed him,' 'I will housebreak him,' etc., but these things take time and effort, and promises can easily be forgotten once the novelty of the new pet has worn off.

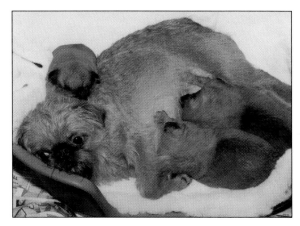

who is virtually helpless in a human world and who trusts his owner for fulfilment of his basic needs for survival. In addition to water and shelter, your pup needs care, protection, guidance and love. If you are not prepared to commit to this, then you are not prepared to own a dog.

Wait a minute, you say. How hard could this be? All of my neighbours own dogs and they seem to be doing just fine. Why should I have to worry about all of this? Well, you should not worry about it; in fact, you will probably find that once your Griffon pup gets used to his new home, he will fall into his place in the family quite naturally. But it never hurts to emphasise the commitment of dog ownership. With some time and patience, it is

Breeders commit considerable time and money in caring for the dam and her puppies. It is no surprise that they seek a responsible, caring owner for their tiny darlings. Do not expect any less of the breeder you choose.

BOY OR GIRL?

An important consideration to be discussed is the sex of your puppy. For a family companion, a bitch may be the better choice, considering the female's inbred concern for all young creatures and her accompanying tolerance and patience. It is always advisable to spay a pet bitch, which may guarantee her a longer life.

A tiny baby Griffon in its breeder's hand, illustrating how delicate and helpless Griffon infants are.

DID YOU KNOW?
You should not even think about buying a puppy that looks sick, undernourished, overly frightened or nervous. Sometimes a timid puppy will warm up to you after a 30-minute 'let's-get-acquainted' session.

really not too difficult to raise a curious and exuberant Griffon pup to be a well-adjusted and well-mannered adult dog—a dog that could be your most loyal friend.

PREPARING PUPPY'S PLACE IN YOUR HOME

Researching your breed and finding a breeder are only two aspects of the 'homework' you will have to do before taking your Griffon puppy home. You will also have to prepare your home and family for the new addition. Much as you would prepare a nursery for a newborn baby, you will need to designate a place in

your home that will be the puppy's own. How you prepare your home will depend on how much freedom the dog will be allowed. Whatever you decide, you must ensure that he has a place that he can 'call his own.'

When you bring your new puppy into your home, you are bringing him into what will become his home as well. Obviously, you did not buy a puppy so that he could take over your house, but in order for a puppy to grow into a stable, well-adjusted dog, he has to feel comfortable in his surroundings. Remember, he is leaving the warmth and security of his mother and littermates, as well as the familiarity of the only place

Water is an essential of all living creatures and should be provided for your Griffon at all times. Keep in mind, when housetraining your Griffon, that what goes in will come out sooner than you expect!

QUALITY FOOD
The cost of food must also be mentioned. All dogs need a good quality food with an adequate supply of protein to develop their bones and muscles properly. Most dogs are not picky eaters but unless fed properly they can quickly succumb to skin problems.

he has ever known, so it is important to make his transition as easy as possible. By preparing a place in your home for the puppy, you are making him feel as welcome as possible in a strange new place. It should not take him long to get used to it, but the sudden shock of being transplanted is somewhat traumatic for a young pup. Imagine how a small child would feel in the same situation—that is how your puppy must be feeling. It is up to you to reassure him and to let him know, 'Little chap, you are going to like it here!'

WHAT YOU SHOULD BUY

CRATE

To someone unfamiliar with the use of crates in dog training, it may seem like punishment to shut

PUPPY PERSONALITY
When a litter becomes available to you, choosing a pup out of all those adorable faces will not be an easy task! Sound temperament is of utmost importance, but each pup has its own personality and some may be better suited to you than others. A feisty, independent pup will do well in a home with older children and adults, while quiet, shy puppies will thrive in a home with minimum noise and distractions. Your breeder knows the pups best and should be able to guide you in the right direction.

YOUR SCHEDULE...
If you lead an erratic, unpredictable life, with daily or weekly changes in your work requirements, consider the problems of owning a puppy. The new puppy has to be fed regularly, socialised (loved, petted, handled, introduced to other people) and, most importantly, allowed to visit outdoors for toilet training. As the dog gets older, it can be more tolerant of deviations in its feeding and toilet relief.

a dog in a crate, but this is not the case at all. Although all breeders do not advocate crate training, more and more breeders and trainers are recommending crates as preferred tools for show puppies as well as pet puppies. Crates are not cruel—crates have many humane and highly effective uses in dog care and

PHOTO COURTESY OF DOSKOCIL

wants to sleep or when he just needs a break. Many dogs sleep in their crates overnight. With soft bedding and his favourite toy, a crate becomes a cosy pseudo-den for your dog. Like his ancestors, he too will seek out the comfort and retreat of a den—you just happen to be providing him with something a little more luxurious than what his early ancestors enjoyed.

As far as purchasing a crate, the type that you buy is up to you. It will most likely be one of the two most popular types: wire or fibreglass. There are advantages and disadvantages to each type. For example, a wire crate is more open, allowing the air to flow through and affording the dog a view of what is going on around him while a fibreglass crate is sturdier. Both can double as travel crates, providing protection for the dog. The size of the crate is another thing to consider. Puppies do not stay puppies forever—in fact, sometimes it seems as if they grow right before your eyes. A small size crate will be necessary for your Griffon, though a medium size crate might be a bit more roomy.

BEDDING
Veterinary bedding in the dog's crate will help the dog feel more at home and you may also like to pop in a small blanket. This will take the place of the leaves, twigs,

Your local pet shop will be able to supply you with a crate suitable for a Griffon.

training. For example, crate training is a very popular and very successful toileting method. A crate can keep your dog safe during travel and, perhaps most importantly, a crate provides your dog with a place of his own in your home. It serves as a 'doggie bedroom' of sorts—your Griffon can curl up in his crate when he etc., that the pup would use in the wild to make a den; the pup can make his own 'burrow' in the crate. Although your pup is far removed from his den-making ancestors, the denning instinct is still a part of his genetic makeup. Second, until you take your pup home, he has been sleeping amidst the warmth of his mother and littermates, and while a blanket is not the same as a warm, breathing body, it still provides heat and something with which to snuggle. You will want to wash your pup's bedding frequently in case he has an accident in his crate, and replace or remove any blanket that becomes ragged and starts to fall apart.

Toys

Toys are a must for dogs of all ages, especially for curious playful pups. Puppies are the 'children' of the dog world, and what child does not love toys? Chew toys provide enjoyment for both dog and owner—your dog will enjoy playing with his favourite toys, while you will enjoy the fact that they distract him from your expensive shoes and leather sofa. Puppies love to chew; in fact, chewing is a physical need for pups as they are teething, and everything looks appetising! The full range of your possessions—from old tea towel to Oriental carpet—are fair game in the eyes of a teething pup.

CRATE TRAINING TIPS

During crate training, you should partition off the section of the crate in which the pup stays. If he is given too big an area, this will hinder your training efforts. Crate training is based on the fact that a dog does not like to soil his sleeping quarters, so it is ineffective to keep a pup in a crate that is so big that he can eliminate in one end and get far enough away from it to sleep. Also, you want to make the crate den-like for the pup. Blankets and a favourite toy will make the crate cosy for the small pup; as he grows, you may want to evict some of his 'roommates' to make more room.

It will take some coaxing at first, but be patient. Given some time to get used to it, your pup will adapt to his new home-within-a-home quite nicely.

Your local pet shop will certainly have a fine variety of leads from which you can choose the one which best suits your needs.

TOYS, TOYS, TOYS!

With a big variety of dog toys available, and so many that look like they would be a lot of fun for a dog, be careful in your selection. It is amazing what a set of puppy teeth can do to an innocent-looking toy, so, obviously, safety is a major consideration. Be sure to choose the most durable products that you can find. Hard nylon bones and toys are a safe bet, and many of them are offered in different scents and flavours that will be sure to capture your dog's attention. It is always fun to play a game of catch with your dog, and there are balls and flying discs that are specially made to withstand dog teeth.

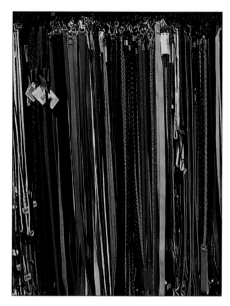

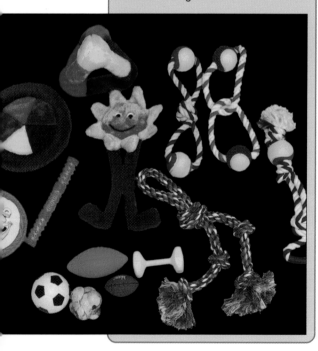

Puppies are not all that discerning when it comes to finding something to literally 'sink their teeth into'—everything tastes great!

Breeders advise owners to resist stuffed toys, because they can become de-stuffed in no time. The overly excited pup may ingest the stuffing, which is neither digestible nor nutritious. Similarly, squeaky toys are quite popular, but must be avoided for the Griffon. Perhaps a squeaky toy can be used as an aid in training, but not for free play. If a pup 'disembowels' one of these, the small plastic squeaker inside can be dangerous if swallowed. Monitor the condition of all your pup's toys carefully and get rid of any that have been chewed to the point of becoming potentially dangerous.

Be careful of natural bones, which have a tendency to splinter into sharp, dangerous pieces. Also be careful of rawhide, which can turn into pieces that are easy to swallow and become a mushy mess on your carpet.

LEAD

A nylon lead is probably the best option as it is the most resistant to puppy teeth should your pup take a liking to chewing on his lead. Of course, this is a habit that should be nipped in the bud, but if your pup likes to chew on his lead he has a very slim chance of being able to chew through the strong

'YOU BETTER SHOP AROUND!'

Finding a reputable breeder that sells healthy pups is very important, but make sure that the breeder you choose is not only someone you respect but also with whom you feel comfortable. Your breeder will be a resource long after you buy your puppy, and you must be able to call with reasonable questions without being made to feel like a pest! If you don't connect on a personal level, investigate some other breeders before making a final decision.

MENTAL AND DENTAL

Toys not only help your puppy get the physical and mental stimulation he needs but also provide a great way to keep his teeth clean. Hard rubber or nylon toys, especially those constructed with grooves, are designed to scrape away plaque, preventing bad breath and gum infection.

nylon. Nylon leads are also lightweight, which is good for a young Griffon who is just getting used to the idea of walking on a lead. For everyday walking and safety purposes, the nylon lead is a good choice. As your pup grows up and gets used to walking on

Your local pet shop sells an array of dishes and bowls suitable for water and food for your Griffon. Get small, shallow bowls or dishes.

PHOTO COURTESY OF MIKKI PET PRODUCTS

the lead, you may want to purchase a flexible lead. These leads allow you to extend the length to give the dog a broader area to explore or to shorten the length to keep the dog near you.

COLLAR

Your pup should get used to wearing a collar all the time since you will want to attach his ID tags to it—plus, you have to attach the lead to something! A lightweight nylon collar is a good choice; make sure that it fits snugly enough so that the pup cannot wriggle out of it, but is loose enough so that it will not be uncomfortably tight around the pup's neck. You should be able to fit a finger between the pup and the collar. It may take some time for your pup to get used to wearing the collar, but soon he will not even notice that it is there.

FOOD AND WATER BOWLS

Your pup will need two bowls, one for food and one for water. You may want two sets of bowls, one for inside and one for outside, depending on where the dog will be fed and where he will be spending time. Stainless steel or sturdy plastic bowls are popular choices. Plastic bowls are more chewable. Dogs tend not to chew on the steel variety, which can be sterilised. It is important to buy sturdy bowls since anything is in

CHOOSE AN APPROPRIATE COLLAR

The **BUCKLE COLLAR** is the standard collar used for everyday purpose. Be sure that you adjust the buckle on growing puppies. Check it every day. It can become too tight overnight! These collars can be made of leather or nylon. Attach your dog's identification tags to this collar.

The **CHOKE COLLAR** is the usual collar recommended for training though it is not ideal for Toy breeds like the Griffon. It is constructed of highly polished steel so that it slides easily through the stainless steel loop. The idea is that the dog controls the pressure around its neck and he will stop pulling if the collar becomes uncomfortable. Never leave a choke collar on your dog when not training.

The **HALTER** is for a trained dog that has to be restrained to prevent running away, chasing a cat and the like. Considered the most humane of all collars, it is frequently used on smaller dogs for which collars are not comfortable.

It is your
responsibility
to clean up
after your
Griffon has
relieved
himself. Pet
shops have
various aids to
assist in the
cleanup job.

danger of being chewed by puppy
teeth and you do not want your
dog to be constantly chewing
apart his bowl (for his safety and
for your purse!).

CLEANING SUPPLIES
Until a pup is housetrained you
will be doing a lot of cleaning.
Accidents will occur, which is
acceptable in the beginning
because the puppy does not know
any better. All you can do is be
prepared to clean up any
'accidents.' Old rags, towels,
newspapers and a safe disinfec-
tant are good to have on hand.

BEYOND THE BASICS
The items previously discussed
are the bare necessities. You will

find out what else you need as
you go along—grooming supplies,
flea/tick protection, baby gates to
partition a room, etc. These things
will vary depending on your
situation but it is important that
you have everything you need to
feed and make your Griffon
comfortable in his first few days at
home.

PUPPY-PROOFING YOUR HOME
Aside from making sure that your
Griffon will be comfortable in
your home, you also have to make
sure that your home is safe for
your Griffon. This means taking
precautions that your pup will not
get into anything he should not
get into and that there is nothing
within his reach that may harm
him should he sniff it, chew it,

HOW VACCINES WORK
If you've just bought a puppy, you
surely know the importance of
having your pup vaccinated, but
do you understand how vaccines
work? Vaccines contain the same
bacteria or viruses that cause the
disease you want to prevent, but
they have been chemically
modified so that they don't cause
any harm. Instead, the vaccine
causes your dog to produce
antibodies that fight the harmful
bacteria. Thus, if your pup is
exposed to the disease in the
future, the antibodies will
destroy the viruses or bacteria.

inspect it, etc. This probably seems obvious since, while you are primarily concerned with your pup's safety, at the same time you do not want your belongings to be ruined. Breakables should be placed out of reach if your dog is to have full run of the house. If he is to be limited to certain places within the house, keep any potentially dangerous items in the 'off-limits' areas. An electrical cord can pose a danger should the puppy decide to taste it—and who is going to convince a pup that it would not make a great chew toy? Cords should be fastened tightly against the wall. If your dog is going to spend time in a crate, make sure that there is nothing near his crate that he can reach if he sticks his curious little nose or paws through the openings. Just as you would with a child, keep all household cleaners and chemicals where the pup cannot reach them.

It is also important to make sure that the outside of your home

NATURAL TOXINS
Examine your grass and garden landscaping before bringing your puppy home. Many varieties of plants have leaves, stems or flowers that are toxic if ingested, and you can depend on a curious puppy to investigate them. Ask your vet for information on poisonous plants or research them at your library.

CHEMICAL TOXINS
Scour your garage for potential puppy dangers. Remove weed killers, pesticides and antifreeze materials. Antifreeze is highly toxic and even a few drops can kill an adult dog. The sweet taste attracts the animal, who will quickly consume it from the floor or curbside.

is safe. Of course your puppy should never be unsupervised, but a pup let loose in the garden will want to run and explore, and he should be granted that freedom. Do not let a fence give you a false sense of security; you would be surprised how crafty (and persistent) a Griffon—with his terrier instincts intact—can be in

TOXIC PLANTS
Many plants can be toxic to dogs. If you see your dog carrying a piece of vegetation in his mouth, approach him in a quiet, disinterested manner, avoid eye contact, pet him and gradually remove the plant from his mouth. Alternatively, offer him a treat and maybe he'll drop the plant on his own accord. Be sure no toxic plants are growing in your own garden.

working out how to dig under and squeeze his way through small holes in a fence. The remedy is to make the fence well embedded into the ground and to be sure to repair or secure any gaps in the fence. Check the fence periodically to ensure that it is in good shape and make repairs as needed; a very determined pup may return to the same spot to

'work on it' until he is able to get through.

FIRST TRIP TO THE VET
You have selected your puppy, and your home and family are ready. Now all you have to do is collect your Griffon from the breeder and the fun begins, right? Well…not so fast. Something else you need to prepare is your pup's first trip to the veterinary surgeon. Perhaps the breeder can recommend someone in the area who specialises in Toy dogs, or maybe you know some other Griffon owners who can suggest a good vet. Either way, you should have an appointment arranged for your pup before you pick him up.

The pup's first visit will consist of an overall examination to make sure that the pup does not have any problems that are not apparent to the owner. The veterinary surgeon will also set up a schedule for the pup's vaccinations; the breeder will inform you of which ones the pup has already received and the vet can continue from there.

INTRODUCTION TO THE FAMILY
Everyone in the house will be excited about the puppy coming home and will want to pet him and play with him, but it is best to make the introduction low-key so as not to overwhelm the puppy. He is apprehensive already. It is the first time he has been

separated from his mother and the breeder, and the ride to your home is likely to be the first time he has been in a car. The last thing you want to do is smother him, as this will only frighten him further. This is not to say that human contact is not extremely necessary at this stage, because this is the time when a connection between the pup and his human family is formed. Gentle petting and soothing words should help console him, as well as just putting him down and letting him explore on his own (under your watchful eye, of course).

The pup may approach the family members or may busy himself with exploring for a while. Gradually, each person should spend some time with the pup, one at a time, crouching down to get as close to the pup's level as possible and letting him sniff their hands and petting him gently. He definitely needs human

Your garden can be overwhelming for your tiny Griffon pup, so be sure to supervise him while he is outdoors.

attention and he needs to be touched—this is how to form an immediate bond. Just remember that the pup is experiencing a lot of things for the first time, at the same time. There are new people, new noises, new smells and new things to investigate: so be gentle, be affectionate and be as comforting as you can be.

PUP'S FIRST NIGHT HOME
You have travelled home with your new charge safely in his crate. He's been to the vet for a thorough check-up; he's been weighed, his papers examined; perhaps he's even been vaccinated and wormed as well. He's met the family, licked the whole family, including the excited children and the less-than-happy cat. He's explored his area, his new bed, the garden and anywhere else he's been permitted. He's eaten his first meal at home and relieved

PUPPY-PROOFING
Thoroughly puppy-proof your house before bringing your puppy home. Never use roach or rodent poisons in any area accessible to the puppy. Avoid the use of toilet cleaners. Most dogs are born with 'toilet sonar' and will take a drink if the lid is left open. Also keep the rubbish secured and out of reach.

the door. Mercifully, he may fall asleep without a peep. When the inevitable occurs, ignore the whining: he is fine. Be strong and keep his interest in mind. Do not allow yourself to feel guilty and visit the pup. He will fall asleep eventually.

Many breeders recommend placing a piece of bedding from his former home in his new bed so that he recognises the scent of his littermates. Others still advise placing a hot water bottle in his bed for warmth. This latter may be a good idea provided the pup doesn't attempt to suckle—he'll get good and wet and may not fall asleep so fast.

Puppy's first night can be somewhat stressful for the pup and his new family. Remember that you are setting the tone of

Whether you adopt a puppy or an adult, your new Griffon will make himself at home in no time.

himself in the proper place. He's heard lots of new sounds, smelled new friends and seen more of the outside world than ever before.

That was just the first day! He's worn out and is ready for bed...or so you think!

It's puppy's first night and you are ready to say 'Good night'— keep in mind that this is puppy's first night ever to be sleeping alone. His dam and littermates are no longer at paw's length and he's a bit scared, cold and lonely. Be reassuring to your new family member. This is not the time to spoil him and give in to his inevitable whining.

Puppies whine. They whine to let others know where they are and hopefully to get company out of it. Place your pup in his new bed or crate in his room and close

---

THE RIDE HOME
Taking your dog from the breeder to your home in a car can be a very uncomfortable experience for both of you. The puppy will have been taken from his warm, friendly, safe environment and brought into a strange new environment. An environment that moves! Be prepared for loose bowels, urination, crying, whining and even fear biting. With proper love and encouragement when you arrive home, the stress of the trip should quickly disappear.

Griffon breeders are a dedicated lot! Once hooked on the Griffon, it is common for owners to adopt a whole pack of them.

PLAY'S THE THING

Teaching the puppy to play with his toys in running and fetching games is an ideal way to help the puppy develop muscle, learn motor skills and bond with you, his owner and master.

He also needs to learn how to inhibit his bite reflex and never to use his teeth on people, forbidden objects and other animals in play. Whenever you play with your puppy, you make the rules. This becomes an important message to your puppy in teaching him that you are the pack leader and control everything he does in life. Once your dog accepts you as his leader, your relationship with him will be cemented for life.

nighttime at your house. Unless you want to play with your pup every evening at 10 p.m., midnight and 2 a.m., don't initiate the habit. Your family will thank you, and so will your pup!

PREVENTING PUPPY PROBLEMS

SOCIALISATION

Now that you have done all of the preparatory work and have helped your pup get accustomed to his new home and family, it is about time for you to have some fun! Socialising your Griffon pup gives you the opportunity to show off your new friend, and your pup gets to reap the benefits of being an adorable furry creature that people will want to pet and, in general, think is absolutely precious!

Besides getting to know his new family, your puppy should be exposed to other people, animals and situations, but of course he must not come into close contact with dogs you don't know well until his course of injections is fully complete. This will help him become well adjusted as he grows up and less prone to being timid or fearful of the new things he will encounter. Your pup's sociali-sation began with the breeder but now it is your responsibility to continue it. The socialisation he receives up until the age of 12 weeks is the most critical, as this is the time when he forms his impressions of the outside world. Be especially careful during the eight-to-ten-week period, also known as the fear period. The interaction he receives during this time should be gentle and reassuring. Lack of socialisation can manifest itself in fear and aggression as the dog grows up. He needs lots of human contact, affection, handling and exposure to other animals.

Once your pup has received his necessary vaccinations, feel free to take him out and about (on his lead, of course). Walk him around the neighbourhood, take him on your daily errands, let people pet him, let him meet other dogs and pets, etc. Puppies do not have to try to make friends; there will be no shortage of people who will want to introduce themselves. Just make sure that you carefully supervise each meeting. If the neighbour-hood children want to say hello, for example, that is great—children and pups most often make great companions. Sometimes an excited child can unintentionally handle a pup too roughly, or an overzealous pup can playfully nip a little too hard. You want to make socialisation experiences positive ones. What a pup learns during this very formative stage will affect his attitude toward future encounters. You want your dog to be comfort-able around everyone. A pup that

SOCIALISATION

Thorough socialisation includes not only meeting new people but also being introduced to new experiences such as riding in the car, having his coat brushed, hearing the television, walking in a crowd—the list is endless. The more your pup experiences, and the more positive the experiences are, the less of a shock and the less frightening it will be for your pup to encounter new things.

has a bad experience with a child may grow up to be a dog that is shy around or aggressive toward children.

CONSISTENCY IN TRAINING

Dogs, being pack animals, naturally need a leader, or else they try to establish dominance in their packs. When you welcome a dog into your family, the choice of who becomes the leader and who becomes the 'pack' is entirely up to you! Your pup's intuitive quest for dominance, coupled with the fact that it is nearly impossible to look at an adorable Griffon pup with his 'puppy-dog' eyes and not cave in, give the pup almost an unfair advantage in getting the

upper hand! A pup will definitely test the waters to see what he can and cannot do. Do not give in to those pleading eyes—stand your ground when it comes to disciplining the pup and make sure that all family members do the same. It will only confuse the pup when Mother tells him to get off the sofa when he is used to sitting up there with Father to watch the nightly news. Avoid discrepancies by having all members of the household decide on the rules before the pup even comes home...and be consistent in enforcing them! Early training shapes the dog's personality, so you cannot be unclear in what you expect.

PROPER SOCIALISATION
The socialisation period for puppies is from age 8 to 16 weeks. This is the time when puppies need to leave their birth family and take up residence with their new owners, where they will meet many new people, other pets, etc. Failure to be adequately socialised can cause the dog to grow up fearing others and being shy and unfriendly due to a lack of self-confidence.

COMMON PUPPY PROBLEMS
The best way to prevent puppy problems is to be proactive in stopping an undesirable behaviour as soon as it starts. The old saying 'You can't teach an old dog new tricks' does not necessarily hold true, but it is true that it is much easier to discourage bad behaviour in a young developing pup than to wait until the pup's bad behaviour becomes the adult dog's bad habit. There are some problems that are especially prevalent in puppies as they develop.

NIPPING
As puppies start to teethe, they feel the need to sink their teeth

into anything available...unfortunately that includes your fingers, arms, hair and toes. You may find this behaviour cute for the first five seconds...until you feel just how sharp those puppy teeth are. This is something you want to discourage immediately and consistently with a firm 'No!' (or whatever number of firm 'No's' it takes for him to understand that you mean business). Then replace your finger with an appropriate chew toy. While this behaviour is merely annoying when the dog is young, it can become dangerous as your Griffon's adult teeth grow in and his jaws develop, and he continues to think it is okay to gnaw on human appendages. Your Griffon does not mean any harm with a friendly nip, but he also does not know his own strength.

CRYING/WHINING

Your pup will often cry, whine, whimper, howl or make some type of commotion when he is left alone. This is basically his way of calling out for attention to make sure that you know he is there and that you have not forgotten about him. He feels insecure when he is left alone, when you are out of the house and he is in his crate or when you are in another part of the house and he cannot see you. The noise he is making is an expression of the anxiety he feels at being alone, so he needs to be taught that being

MANNERS MATTER
During the socialisation process, a puppy should meet people, experience different environments and definitely be exposed to other canines. Through playing and interacting with other dogs, your puppy will learn lessons, ranging from controlling the pressure of his jaws by biting his littermates to the inner-workings of the canine pack that he will apply to his human relationships for the rest of his life. That is why removing a puppy from its litter too early (before eight weeks) can be detrimental to the pup's development.

Before buying a Griffon puppy, or any other puppy for that matter, be certain that you have the time and inclination to properly train and care for the dog as it grows.

alone is okay. You are not actually training the dog to stop making noise, you are training him to feel comfortable when he is alone and thus removing the need for him to make the noise. This is where the crate with cosy bedding and a toy comes in handy. You want to know that he is safe when you are not there to supervise, and you know that he will be safe in his crate rather than roaming freely about the house. In order for the pup to stay in his crate without making a fuss, he needs to be comfortable in his crate. On that note, it is extremely important that the crate is never used as a form of punishment, or the pup will have a negative association with the crate.

Accustom the pup to the crate in short, gradually increasing time intervals in which you put him in the crate, maybe with a treat, and stay in the room with him. If he cries or makes a fuss, do not go to him, but stay in his sight. Gradually he will realise that staying in his crate is all right without your help, and it will not be so traumatic for him when you

NO CHOCOLATE!
Use treats to bribe your dog into a desired behaviour. Try small pieces of hard cheese or freeze-dried liver. Never offer chocolate as it has toxic qualities for dogs.

CHEWING TIPS
Chewing goes hand in hand with nipping in the sense that a teething puppy is always looking for a way to soothe his aching gums. In this case, instead of chewing on you, he may have taken a liking to your favourite shoe or something else which he should not be chewing. Again, realise that this is a normal canine behaviour that does not need to be discouraged, only redirected. Your pup just needs to be taught what is acceptable to chew on and what is off limits. Consistently tell him 'NO' when you catch him chewing on something forbidden and give him a chew toy. Conversely, praise him when you catch him chewing on something appropriate. In this way you are discouraging the inappropriate behaviour and reinforcing the desired behaviour. The puppy chewing should stop after his adult teeth have come in, but an adult dog continues to chew for various reasons—perhaps because he is bored, perhaps to relieve tension or perhaps he just likes to chew. That is why it is important to redirect his chewing when he is still young.

are not around. You may want to leave the radio on softly when you leave the house; the sound of human voices may be comforting to him.

FEEDING YOUR GRIFFON

SPECIAL FEEDING CONSIDERATIONS

A Griffon should be fed sensibly on a high-quality diet, but an owner should never be tempted to allow the dog to put on too much weight, for an overweight dog is more prone to health problems than one that is of the correct weight for its size.

> **FEEDING TIP**
> You must store your dried dog food carefully. Open packages of dog food quickly lose their vitamin value, usually within 90 days of being opened. Mould spores and vermin could also contaminate the food.

Most owners like to feed two small meals each day, but, however frequently you decide to feed your dog, remember that no dog should ever be fed within an hour of strenuous exercise.

If you have chosen your breeder well, you should be able to obtain sound advice from that breeder as to which food he considers most suitable. When you buy your puppy, the breeder should have provided you with a diet sheet giving details of exactly how your puppy has been fed. Of course you will be at liberty to change that food, together with the frequency and timing of meals, as the youngster reaches adulthood, but this should be done gradually.

It is important that small dogs, if fed on proprietary foods, have 'small bites' for they will not be able to cope well with larger pieces. Some breeders also like to soak the food before feeding, especially if teeth are missing or loose, as might be the case in older animals.

Every breeder will have his preference with regard to selection of food, but after the age of six months many select a lower protein diet than was given during the early months of life.

Several Griffon owners prefer to feed fresh food, instead of one of the more convenient complete diets. Minced beef is very popular and can be fed raw or cooked, whichever the dog prefers. Other meats such as heart, ox cheek, mutton or liver are also suitable, but the latter should only be fed in moderation for too much can cause loose motions. Obviously small mouths will need the meat cut up into small pieces, even though many Griffons would be perfectly prepared to tackle a large joint if given the opportunity! Too much dairy content is not wise, but small amounts of cheese, scrambled or boiled eggs are also appreciated, as is the occasional portion of fruit. Fish may also be given, but, of course, extreme care must be taken to remove all bones, as is the case with chicken and rabbit.

When feeding dried biscuits as a snack, it is wisest to buy

FOOD PREFERENCE

Selecting the best dried dog food is difficult. There is no majority consensus among veterinary scientists as to the value of nutrient analyses (protein, fat, fibre, moisture, ash, cholesterol, minerals, etc.). All agree that feeding trials are what matters, but you also have to consider the individual dog. Its weight, age, activity and what pleases its taste, all must be considered. It is probably best to take the advice of your veterinary surgeon. Every dog's dietary requirements vary, even during the lifetime of a particular dog.

If your dog is fed a good dried food, it does not require supplements of meat or vegetables. Dogs do appreciate a little variety in their diets so you may choose to stay with the same brand, but vary the flavour. Alternatively you may wish to add a little flavoured stock to give a difference to the taste.

TEST FOR PROPER DIET

A good test for proper diet is the colour, odour and firmness of your dog's stool. A healthy dog usually produces three semi-hard stools per day. The stools should have no unpleasant odour. They should be the same colour from excretion to excretion.

THE CANINE GOURMET

Your dog does not prefer a fresh bone. Indeed, he wants it properly aged and, if given such a treat indoors, he is more likely to try to bury it in the carpet than he is to settle in for a good chew! If you have a garden, give him such delicacies outside and guide him to a place suitable for his 'bone yard.' He will carefully place the treasure in its earthy vault and seemingly forget about it. Trust me, his seeming distaste or lack of thanks for your thoughtfulness is not that at all. He will return in a few days to inspect it, perhaps to re-bury the thing, and when it is just right, he will relish it as much as you do that cooked-to-perfection steak. If he is in a concrete or bricked kennel run, he will be especially frustrated at the hopelessness of the situation. He will vacillate between ignoring it completely, giving it a few licks to speed the curing process with saliva, and trying to hide it behind the water bowl! When the bone has aged a bit, he will set to work on it.

small ones, or to break them up into smallish pieces, especially for youngsters.

FOOD CHOICES

Today the choices of food for your Griffon are many and varied. There are simply dozens of brands of food in all sorts of flavours and textures, ranging from puppy diets to those for seniors. There are even hypoallergenic and low-calorie diets available. Because your Griffon's food has a bearing on coat, health and temperament, it is essential that the most suitable diet is selected for a Griffon of his age. It is fair to say, however, that even experienced owners can be perplexed by the enormous range of foods available. Only understanding what is best for your dog will help you reach a valued decision.

Dog foods are produced in three basic types: dried, semi-moist and tinned. Dried foods are useful for the cost-conscious for overall they tend to be less expensive than semi-moist or tinned. They also contain the least fat and the most preservatives. In general, tinned foods are made up of 60–70 percent water, while semi-moist ones often contain so much sugar that they are perhaps the least preferred by owners, even though their dogs seem to like them.

When selecting your dog's diet, three stages of development

must be considered: the puppy stage, adult stage and the senior or veteran stage.

PUPPY STAGE

Puppies instinctively want to suck milk from their mother's teats and a normal puppy will exhibit this behaviour from just a few moments following birth. If puppies do not attempt to suckle within the first half-hour or so, they should be encouraged to do so by placing them on the nipples, having selected ones with plenty of milk. This early milk supply is important in providing colostrum

GRAIN-BASED DIETS

Some less expensive dog foods are based on grains and other plant proteins. While these products may appear to be attractively priced, many breeders prefer a diet based on animal proteins and believe that they are more conducive to your dog's health. Many grain-based diets rely on soy protein that may cause flatulence (passing gas).

There are many cases, however, when your dog might require a special diet. These special requirements should only be recommended by your veterinary surgeon.

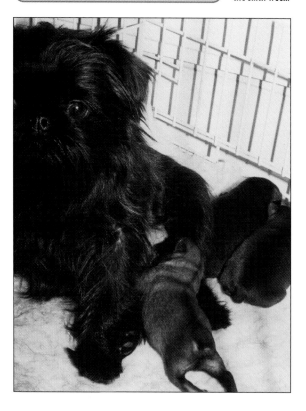

A black rough dam with her one-week-old puppies. There is no better food for puppies than their mother's milk. The breeder begins weaning by the sixth week.

FEEDING TIP

Dog food must be at room temperature, neither too hot nor too cold. Fresh water, changed daily and served in a clean bowl, is mandatory, especially when feeding dried food.

Never feed your dog from the table while you are eating. Never feed your dog leftovers from your own meal. They usually contain too much fat and too much seasoning.

Dogs must chew their food. Hard pellets are excellent; soups and slurries are to be avoided.

Don't add left-overs or any extras to normal dog food. The normal food is usually balanced and adding something extra destroys the balance.

Except for age-related changes, dogs do not require dietary variations. They can be fed the same diet, day after day, without their becoming ill.

DRINK, DRANK, DRUNK —MAKE IT A DOUBLE

In both humans and dogs, as well as most living organisms, water forms the major part of nearly every body tissue. Naturally, we take water for granted, but without it, life as we know it would cease.

For dogs, water is needed to keep their bodies functioning biochemically. Additionally, water is needed to replace the water lost while panting. Unlike humans who are able to sweat to dissipate heat, dogs must pant to cool down, thereby losing the vital water from their bodies needed to regulate their body temperatures. Humans lose electrolyte-containing products and other body-fluid components through sweating; dogs do not lose anything except water.

Water is essential always, but especially so when the weather is hot or humid or when your dog is exercising or working vigorously.

to protect the puppies during the first eight to ten weeks of their lives. Although a mother's milk is much better than any milk formula, despite there being some excellent ones available, if the puppies do not feed, the breeder will have to feed them himself. For those with less experience, advice from a veterinary surgeon is important so that you feed not only the right quantity of milk but that of correct quality, fed at

suitably frequent intervals, usually every two hours during the first few days of life.

Puppies should be allowed to nurse from their mothers for about the first six weeks, although from the third or fourth week you should begin to introduce small portions of suitable solid food. Most breeders like to introduce alternate milk and meat meals initially, building up to weaning time.

By the time the puppies are seven or a maximum of eight weeks old, they should be fully weaned and fed solely on a proprietary puppy food. Selection of the most suitable, good-quality diet at this time is essential, for a puppy's fastest growth rate is during the first year of life. Veterinary surgeons are usually able to offer advice in this regard and, although the frequency of meals will have been reduced over time, only when a young dog has reached the age of about 12 months should an adult diet be fed.

Puppy and junior diets should be well balanced for the needs of your dog, so that except in certain circumstances additional vitamins, minerals and proteins will not be required.

ADULT DIETS

A dog is considered an adult when it has stopped growing, so in general the diet of a Griffon can

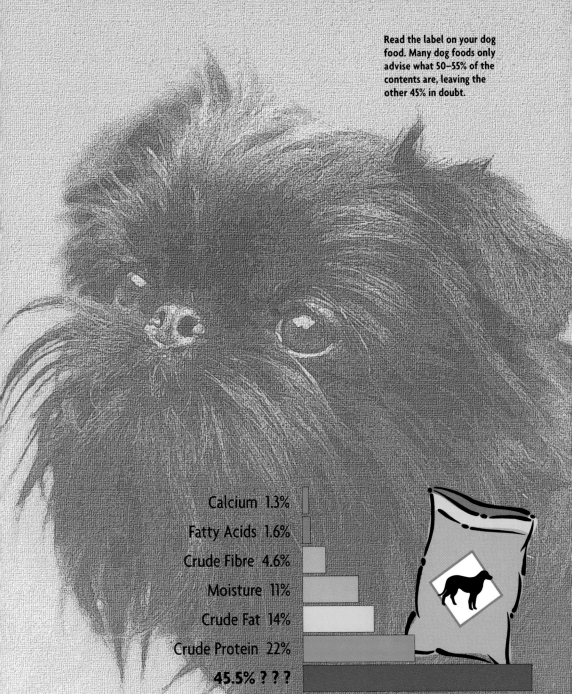

be changed to an adult one at about 10 to 12 months of age. Again you should rely upon your veterinary surgeon or dietary specialist to recommend an acceptable maintenance diet. Major dog food manufacturers specialise in this type of food, and it is merely necessary for you to select the one best suited to your dog's needs. Active dogs may have different requirements than sedate dogs.

SENIOR DIETS

As dogs get older, their metabolism changes. The older dog usually exercises less, moves more slowly and sleeps more. This change in lifestyle and physiological performance requires a change in diet. Since

> **'DOES THIS COLLAR MAKE ME LOOK FAT?'**
> While humans may obsess about how they look and how trim their bodies are, many people believe that extra weight on their dogs is a good thing. The truth is, pets should not be over- or under-weight, as both can lead to or signal sickness. In order to tell how fit your pet is, run your hands over his ribs. Are his ribs buried under a layer of fat or are they sticking out considerably? If your pet is within his normal weight range, you should be able to feel the ribs easily. If you stand above him, the outline of his body should resemble an hourglass. Some breeds do tend to be leaner while some are a bit stockier, but making sure your dog is the right weight for his breed will certainly contribute to his good health.

Before offering your Griffon puppy milk, consult with your breeder or vet. All puppies cannot tolerate cow's or goat's milk as naturally as they accept their mother's own milk.

these changes take place slowly, they might not be recognisable. What is easily recognisable is weight gain. By continuing to feed your dog an adult-maintenance diet when it is slowing down metabolically, your dog will gain weight. Obesity in an older dog compounds the health problems that already accompany old age.

As your dog gets older, few of his organs function up to par. The kidneys slow down and the intestines become less efficient. These age-related factors are best handled with a change in diet and a change in feeding schedule to give smaller portions that are more easily digested.

There is no single best diet for every older dog. While many dogs do well on light or senior diets, other dogs do better on puppy diets or other special premium diets such as lamb and rice. Be sensitive to your senior Griffon's diet and this will help control other problems that may arise with your old friend.

WATER

Just as your dog needs proper nutrition from his food, water is an essential 'nutrient' as well. Water keeps the dog's body properly hydrated and promotes normal function of the body's systems. During housetraining it is necessary to keep an eye on how much water your Griffon is drinking, but once he is reliably

TIPPING THE SCALES
Good nutrition is vital to your dog's health, but many people end up over-feeding or giving unnecessary supple-ments. Here are some common doggie diet don'ts:
• Adding milk, yoghurt and cheese to your dog's diet may seem like a good idea for coat and skin care, but dairy products are very fattening and can cause indigestion.
• Diets high in fat will not cause heart attacks in dogs but will certainly cause your dog to gain weight.
• Most importantly, don't assume your dog will simply stop eating once he doesn't need any more food. Given the chance, he will eat you out of house and home!

trained he should have access to clean fresh water at all times, especially if you feed dried food. Make certain that the dog's water bowl is clean, and change the water often.

EXERCISE

Griffons, although small, are an active breed that thoroughly enjoys exercise. Adults will usually be more than happy to be taken for lead walks, and will also enjoy free run, though owners should be careful that the areas in which their dogs exercise are thoroughly safe. Keep in mind, too, that Griffons do tend to like other dogs, but seem to have no idea that their own size is somewhat diminutive. Although not aggressive, they will stand their ground, so owners should be sensible when meeting dogs whose temperament is unknown to them.

Griffons living in homes with gardens will exercise themselves quite happily in their own grounds, especially if more than one dog is kept in the family, but do keep in mind that they are frequently good diggers! Take care, too, that your inquisitive Griffon does not have access to any plants or other things around the garden that

CHANGE IN DIET
As your dog's caretaker, you know the importance of keeping his diet consistent, but sometimes when you run out of food or if you're on holiday, you have to make a change quickly. Some dogs will experience digestive problems, but most will not. If you are planning on changing your dog's menu, do so gradually to ensure that your dog will not have any problems. Over a period of four to five days, slowly add some new food to your dog's old food, increasing the percentage of new food each day.

might contain poisons.

To keep any breed of dog in healthy bodily condition, it is essential that opportunity be given to build up muscle tone. This important part of canine care should never be overlooked, even in a breed as small as the Griffon Bruxellois.

DO DOGS HAVE TASTE BUDS?
Watching a dog 'wolf' or gobble his food, seemingly without chewing, leads an owner to wonder whether their dogs can taste anything. Yes, dogs have taste buds, with sensory perception of sweet, salty and sour. Puppies are born with fully mature taste buds.

GROOMING
There is a very important difference in coat care requirements for a rough-coated Griffon and a smooth. The latter requires much less work, principally just the occasional bath and regular brushing with a bristle brush, which also tones the skin. Any strands of loose hair around the anus and tail will need to be trimmed neatly, and it is

LET THE SUN SHINE

Your dog needs daily sunshine for the same reason people do. Pets kept inside homes with curtains drawn against the sun suffer 'SAD' (Seasonal Affected Disorder) to the same degree as humans. We now know that sunlight must enter the iris and thus to the pineal gland to regulate the body's hormonal system and when we live and work in artificial light, both circadian rhythms and hormone balances are disturbed.

important to keep eyes, ears and face thoroughly clean. Although a smooth Griffon's coat is short, whether or not it has been well looked after will always be apparent. A smooth Griffon generally sheds coat twice per year, at which time a comb is useful too, for this aids the removal of dead hair.

Dealing with the coat of a rough-coated Griffon is quite different as the coat will need hand stripping, usually twice a year. Although it is infinitely better to hand strip, some pet owners have their Griffons clipped at a parlour. However, this will change the texture of the coat, as well as the colour, and is certainly not suitable for any Griffon whose destiny lies in the show ring.

A rough-coated Griffon will need to learn to be patient while being stripped, so from a young age it is wise to get a puppy into the habit of sitting quietly on a table. A puppy will be ready to have its first light trim when about three or four months old. Coats vary and some puppies have rather a soft puppy coat that is more difficult to take out, so will take even more patience on the puppy's part! The soft hair needs to be removed to encourage coarser hair to grow in its place.

STRIPPING

Most Griffon owners begin by thoroughly combing the coat. Then, steadying the dog with one hand while also keeping the skin taut, finger and thumb of the free

The feel of a brush on the young pup's coat takes some getting used to. Introduce the puppy to grooming right away and he will soon grow to enjoy it.

Your local pet shop will have a variety of grooming tools from which you may select those most useful in grooming your Griffon.

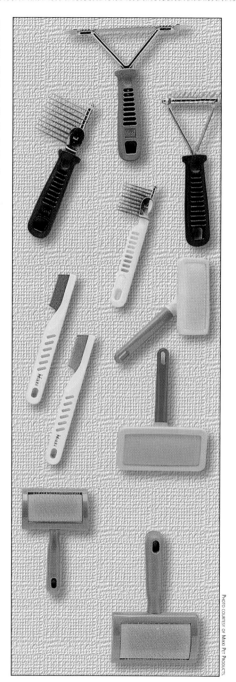

PHOTO COURTESY OF MIKKI PET PRODUCTS.

hand are used to lift the dead coat so that a few hairs can be taken out at a time. Always pull in the direction of coat growth, and pull only at the hair, not at the skin. Provided that the coat is ready to be stripped, this is not as uncomfortable for the dog as it sounds, for the hairs come out easily and the dog feels no pain at all.

Stripping is usually commenced along the back, always removing only a few hairs at a time. Most people prefer to leave in the undercoat until the harsh hairs re-grow; later they remove the old undercoat, when it is looking lighter than its usual colour and is softer than normal. Taking both coats out together will result in a very sparsely

GROOMING EQUIPMENT

How much grooming equipment you purchase will depend on how much grooming you are going to do. Here are some basics:

• Natural bristle brush
• Slicker brush
• Metal comb
• Scissors
• Blaster
• Rubber mat
• Dog shampoo
• Spray hose attachment
• Ear cleaner
• Cotton wipes
• Towels
• Nail clippers

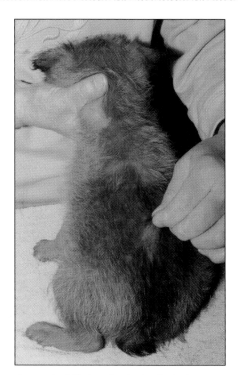

A puppy should be introduced to hand stripping at a young age. Gradually the puppy will accept this grooming method and remain cooperative. Hand stripping is a painless procedure, though it is wise to learn the stripping process from your breeder or a professional groomer or Griffon handler.

coated dog, added to which, the dog could catch cold!

The usual order of stripping is the back, followed by neck and head, then chest and hindquarters. Under the tummy the skin is more delicate, so some breeders prefer to strip where it will not cause pain, and use trimming scissors in areas likely to be more tender.

The head area needs very careful attention. Top and sides are stripped to eye level, but the beard is allowed to grow. Hair on earflaps should be stripped gently because this is a particularly delicate area, but hair on the ears is to be left as short as possible. Hair inside the ear can also be removed.

The tail is usually one of the final parts of the dog to be stripped. Some of the longer hairs are often trimmed with scissors, because again this can be somewhat sensitive, especially around the base of the tail; indeed much more sensitive than on legs and body where hair is easy to strip out. As much hair as possible is taken off the feet, and then the foot is trimmed so that the foot shows its neat, rounded cat-like shape. Remember that hair also grows under the pads of the feet, so this will also need to be trimmed.

Hand stripping the back of an adult Griffon removes the dead hair and leaves the desirable rough coat.

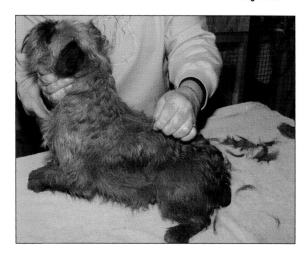

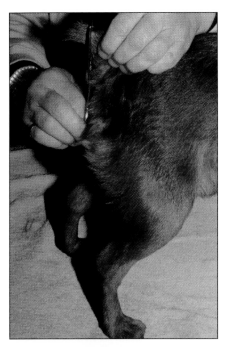

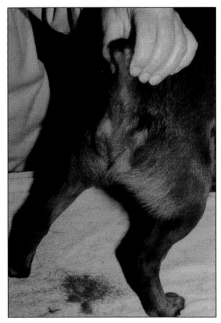

The hair on the tail should be cut with scissors to give it a tidy appearance. The lower photo shows a properly trimmed tail.

GENERAL TIDYING

Other than when carrying out a complete strip, the coat of a rough Griffon will need to be tidied periodically so that it never gets out of hand. The beard should be regularly checked to see that food has not become entangled. It is a simple procedure to sponge the beard and then comb it through.

BATHING

Dogs do not need to be bathed as often as humans, but regular bathing is essential for healthy skin and a healthy, shiny coat. Again, like most anything, if you accustom your pup to being bathed as a puppy, it will be second nature by the time he grows up. You want your dog to be at ease in the bath or else it could end up a wet, soapy, messy ordeal for both of you!

Brush your Griffon thoroughly before wetting his coat. This will get rid of most mats and tangles, which are harder to remove when the coat is wet. Make certain that your dog has a good non-slip surface to stand on. Begin by wetting the dog's coat. A shower or hose attachment is necessary for thoroughly wetting and rinsing the coat. Check the water temperature to make sure that it is neither too hot nor too cold.

Next, apply shampoo to the dog's coat and work it into a good lather. You should purchase a shampoo that is made for dogs. Do

SOAP IT UP

The use of human soap products like shampoo, bubble bath and hand soap can be damaging to a dog's coat and skin. Human products are too strong and remove the protective oils coating the dog's hair and skin (making him water-resistant). Use only shampoo made especially for dogs and you may like to use a medicated shampoo, which will always help to keep external parasites at bay.

not use a product made for human hair. Wash the head last; you do not want shampoo to drip into the dog's eyes while you are washing the rest of his body. Work the shampoo all the way down to the skin. You can use this opportunity to check the skin for any bumps, bites or other abnormalities. Do not neglect any area of the body— get all of the hard-to-reach places.

Once the dog has been thoroughly shampooed, he requires an equally thorough rinsing. Shampoo left in the coat can be irritating to the skin. Protect his eyes from the shampoo by shielding them with your hand and directing the flow of water in the opposite direction. You should also avoid getting water in the ear canal. Be prepared for your dog to shake out his coat— you might want to stand back, but

make sure you have a hold on the dog to keep him from running through the house.

NAILS

Never forget that toenails should be kept short, both on rough-coated dogs and on smooths. Canine nail clippers can easily be obtained from pet shops, and many owners find those of the 'guillotine' design easier to use.

Grooming is simpler if you have a grooming table on which to place your Griffon.

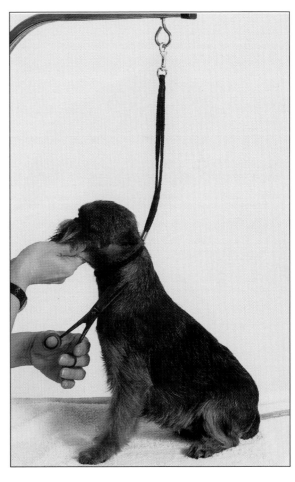

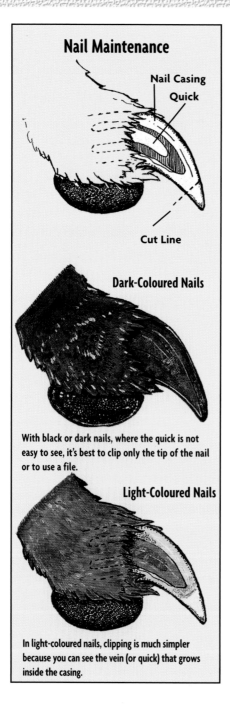

Nail Maintenance

Nail Casing

Quick

Cut Line

Dark-Coloured Nails

With black or dark nails, where the quick is not easy to see, it's best to clip only the tip of the nail or to use a file.

Light-Coloured Nails

In light-coloured nails, clipping is much simpler because you can see the vein (or quick) that grows inside the casing.

BATHING BEAUTY

Once you are sure that the dog is thoroughly rinsed, squeeze the excess water out of the coat with your hand and dry him with a heavy towel. You may choose to use a blaster on his coat or just let it dry naturally. In cold weather, never allow your dog outside with a wet coat.

There are 'dry bath' products on the market, which are sprays and powders intended for spot cleaning, that can be used between regular baths, if necessary. They are not substitutes for regular baths, but they are easy to use for touch-ups as they do not require rinsing.

Your Griffon should be accustomed to having his nails trimmed at an early age, since it will be part of your maintenance routine throughout his life. Not only does it look nicer, but long nails can scratch someone unintentionally. Also, a long nail has a better chance of ripping and bleeding, or causing the feet to spread. A good rule of thumb is that if you can hear your dog's nails clicking on the floor when he walks, his nails are too long.

Before you start cutting, make sure you can identify the 'quick' in each nail. The quick is a blood vessel that runs through the centre of each nail and grows rather close to the end. It will bleed if accidentally cut, which will be quite painful for the dog as it contains nerve endings. Keep some type of clotting agent on hand, such as a styptic pencil or styptic powder (the type used for shaving). This will stop the bleeding quickly when applied to the end of the cut nail. Do not panic if you cut the quick, just stop the bleeding and talk soothingly to your dog. Once he has calmed down, move on to the next nail. It is better to clip a little at a time, particularly with black-nailed dogs.

Hold your pup steady as you begin trimming his nails; you do not want him to make any sudden movements or run away. Talk to him soothingly and stroke him as you clip. Holding his foot in your hand, simply take off the end of each nail in one quick clip.

Nose

If a Griffon develops a rather dry nose, a little grease or butter can be applied to remedy this. (However, always keep in the back of your mind that a dry nose might also be a sign of illness.)

Eyes

On rough Griffons great care should be taken to keep the eyes clear of hair, so that it does not get into the eyes causing aggravation, leading to long-term injury. Owners use different methods, either pulling the hairs out very carefully or cutting the hairs away

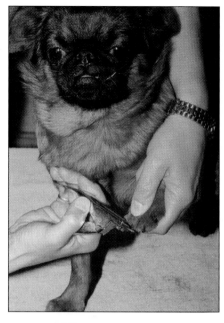

The nails are clipped with a special guillo-tine-type clipper made especially for dog's nails.

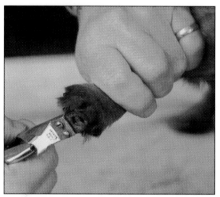

The guillotine clippers are the most popular because they are easy to use and safe for the dog.

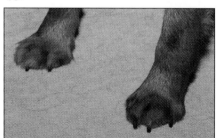

Front paws should look tidy with short nails.

The Griffon's tear stains can be cleaned with a soft wipe and a tear-stain remover available from your local pet shop.

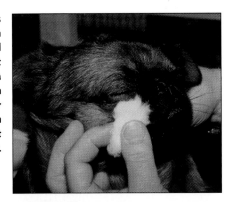

The Griffon's ears are cleaned with a soft cotton wipe and ear cleaning powder available from your local pet shop.

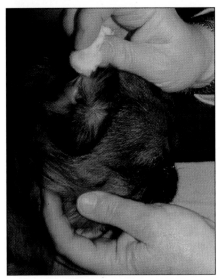

Don't forget to brush your Griffon's teeth at least once per week. Your pet shop sells doggy tooth-paste and toothbrushes, often in a combination package.

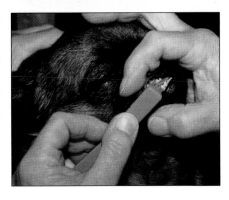

with a suitable pair of scissors. Naturally extreme care is absolutely essential when grooming near the eyes, for accidents can all too easily happen.

EAR CARE

Ears should be kept clean using a special cleaner, but take care not to delve too deeply into the ear canal as this might cause injury. Be on the lookout for any signs of infection or ear mite infestation. If your Griffon has been shaking his head or scratching at his ears frequently, this usually indicates a problem. If his ears have an unusual odour, this is a sure sign of mite infestation or infection, and a signal to have his ears checked by the veterinary surgeon.

TEETH

Teeth should always be kept as free from tartar as possible. There are now several canine tooth-cleaning agents available, including the basics, like a small toothbrush and canine toothpaste.

ANAL GLANDS

Most owners of pet dogs prefer to have anal glands checked by a vet, either on a routine visit, or when a dog is showing any kind of discomfort around the rear end. However, most breeders deal with anal glands themselves, for this is a reasonably simple procedure.

The glands are located on either side of the anus so, holding the tail up with one hand, one can gently squeeze the glands with finger and thumb of the other. It is imperative to hold a tissue or wad of cotton-wool at the sight of evacuation, for the resultant discharge not only smells unpleasant but is not a pretty sight!

TRAVELLING WITH YOUR DOG

CAR TRAVEL

You should accustom your Griffon to riding in a car at an early age. You may or may not take him in the car often, but at the very least he will need to go to the vet and you do not want these trips to be traumatic for the dog or troublesome for you. The safest way for a dog to ride in the car is in his crate. If he uses a crate in the house, you can use the same crate for travel.

Put the pup in the crate and see how he reacts. If he seems uneasy, you can have a passenger hold him on his lap while you drive. Another option is a specially made safety harness for dogs, which straps the dog in much like a seat belt. Do not let the dog roam loose in the vehicle—this is very dangerous! If you should stop short, your dog can be thrown and injured. If the dog starts climbing on you and pestering you while you are

> **PEDICURE TIP**
> A dog that spends a lot of time outside on a hard surface, such as cement or pavement, will have his nails naturally worn down and may not need to have them trimmed as often, except maybe in the colder months when he is not outside as much. Regardless, it is best to get your dog accustomed to this procedure at an early age so that he is used to it. Some dogs are especially sensitive about having their feet touched, but if a dog has experienced it since he was young, he should not be bothered by it.

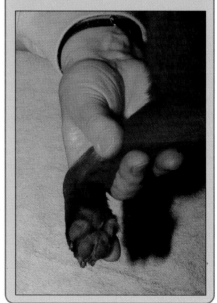

driving, you will not be able to concentrate on the road. It is an unsafe situation for everyone— human and canine.

For long trips, be prepared to

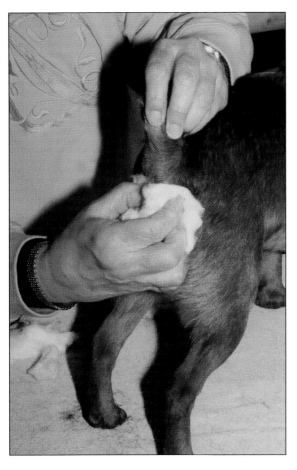

fairly unusual and advance permission is always required. The dog will be required to travel in a fibreglass crate and you should always check in advance with the airline regarding specific requirements. To help the dog be at ease, put one of his favourite toys in the crate with him. Do not feed the dog for at least six hours before the trip to minimise his need to relieve himself. However, certain regulations specify that water must always be made available to the dog in the crate.

Make sure your dog is properly identified and that your contact information appears on his ID tags and on his crate. Animals travel in a different area of the plane than human passengers so every rule must be strictly followed so as to prevent the risk of getting separated from your dog. Since the Griffon is such a small tyke of a dog, it is advisable to enquire whether the airline permits Toy dogs to travel as 'carry-ons.'

Although not a pleasant procedure (for the owner), expressing the anal glands is not difficult, but the procedure is probably best left for the veterinary surgeon.

stop to let the dog relieve himself. Take with you whatever you need to clean up after him, including some paper kitchen towels and perhaps some old towelling for use should he have an accident in the car or suffer from travel sickness.

AIR TRAVEL
While it is possible to take a dog on a flight within Britain, this is

ON THE ROAD
If you are going on a long motor trip with your dog, be sure the hotels are dog friendly. Many hotels do not accept dogs. Also take along some ice that can be thawed and offered to your dog if he becomes overheated. Most dogs like to lick ice.

TRAVEL TIP

The most extensive travel you do with your dog may be limited to trips to the veterinary surgeon's office—or you may decide to bring him along for long distances when the family goes on holiday. Whichever the case, it is important to consider your dog's safety while travelling.

BOARDING

So you want to take a family holiday—and you want to include all members of the family. You would probably make arrangements for accommodation ahead of time anyway, but this is especially important when travelling with a dog. You do not want to make an overnight stop at the only place around for miles and find out that they do not allow dogs. Also, you do not want to reserve a place for your family without confirming that you are travelling with a dog because if it is against their policy you may not have a place to stay.

Alternatively, if you are travelling and choose not to bring your Griffon, you will have to make arrangements for him while you are away. Some options are to take him to a neighbour's house to stay while you are gone, to have a trusted neighbour pop in often or stay at your house, or bring your dog to a reputable boarding kennel. If you choose to board him at a kennel, you should visit in advance to see the facilities provided, how clean they are and where the dogs are kept. Talk to some of the employees and see how they treat the dogs—do they spend time with the dogs, play with them, exercise them, etc.? Also find out the kennel's policy on vaccinations and what they require. This is for all of the dogs' safety, since when dogs are kept

Leaving your Griffons home is never easy, but if your dogs cannot join you on your holiday, it is wise to find a quality boarding facility with which you feel confident.

It is best to locate a kennel before you actually require one in which to board your Griffon. Reservations should be made as far in advance as possible.

together, there is a greater risk of diseases being passed from dog to dog.

IDENTIFICATION

Your Griffon is your valued companion and friend. That is why you always keep a close eye on him and you have made sure that he cannot escape from the garden or wriggle out of his collar and run away from you. However, accidents can happen and there may come a time when your dog unexpectedly gets separated from you. If this unfortunate event should occur, the first thing on your mind will be finding him. Proper identification, including an ID tag, a tattoo and possibly a

microchip, will increase the chances of his being returned to you safely and quickly.

VACCINATIONS

For international travel you will have to make arrangements well in advance (perhaps months), as countries' regulations pertaining to bringing in animals differ. There may be special health certificates and/or vaccinations that your dog will need before taking the trip; sometimes this has to be done within a certain time frame. In rabies-free countries, you will need to bring proof of the dog's rabies vaccination and there may be a quarantine period upon arrival.

IDENTIFICATION OPTIONS

As puppies become more and more expensive, especially those puppies of high quality for showing and/or breeding, they have a greater chance of being stolen. The usual collar dog tag is, of course, easily removed. But there are two techniques that have become widely used for identification.

The puppy microchip implantation involves the injection of a small microchip, about the size of a corn kernel, under the skin of the dog. If your dog shows up at a clinic or shelter, or is offered for resale under less than savoury circumstances, it can be positively identified by the microchip. The microchip is scanned and a registry quickly identifies you as the owner. This is not only protection against theft, but should the dog run away or go chasing a squirrel and get lost, you have a fair chance of getting it back.

Tattooing is done on various parts of the dog, from its belly to its cheeks. The number tattooed can be your telephone number or any other number which you can easily memorise. When professional dog thieves see a tattooed dog, they usually lose interest in it. Both microchipping and tattooing can be done at your local veterinary clinic. For the safety of our dogs, no laboratory facility or dog broker will accept a tattooed dog as stock.

IDENTIFICATION TAGS

If your dog gets lost, he is not able to ask for directions home.

Identification tags fastened to the collar give important information—the dog's name, the owner's name, the owner's address and a telephone number where the owner can be reached. This makes it easy for whomever finds the dog to contact the owner and arrange to have the dog returned. An added advantage is that a person will be more likely to approach a lost dog who has ID tags on his collar; it tells the person that this is somebody's pet rather than a stray. This is the easiest and fastest method of identification provided that the tags stay on the collar and the collar stays on the dog.

Your Griffon should never be without a light collar and his identification tag.

Living with an untrained dog is a lot like owning a piano that you do not know how to play—it is a nice object to look at but it does not do much more than that to bring you pleasure. Now try taking piano lessons and suddenly the piano comes alive and brings forth magical sounds and rhythms that set your heart singing and your body swaying.

The same is true with your Griffon. Any dog is a big responsibility and if not trained sensibly may develop unacceptable behaviour that annoys you or could even cause family friction.

To train your Griffon, you may like to enrol in an obedience

REAP THE REWARDS
If you start with a normal, healthy dog and give him time, patience and some carefully executed lessons, you will reap the rewards of that training for the life of the dog. And what a life it will be! The two of you will find immeasurable pleasure in the companionship you have built together with love, respect and understanding.

class. Teach him good manners as you learn how and why he behaves the way he does. Find out how to communicate with your dog and how to recognise and understand his communications with you. Suddenly the dog takes on a new role in your life— he is clever, interesting, well-behaved and fun to be with. He demonstrates his bond of devotion to you daily. In other words, your Griffon does wonders for your ego because he constantly reminds you that you are not only his leader, you are his hero!

PARENTAL GUIDANCE
Training a dog is a life experience. Many parents admit that much of what they know about raising children they learned from caring for their dogs. Dogs respond to love, fairness and guidance, just as children do. Become a good dog owner and you may become an even better parent.

Those involved with teaching dog obedience and counselling owners about their dogs' behaviour have discovered some interesting facts about dog ownership. For example, training dogs when they are puppies results in the highest rate of success in developing well-mannered and well-adjusted adult dogs. Training an older dog, from six months to six years of age, can produce almost equal results providing that the owner accepts the dog's slower rate of learning capability and is willing to work patiently to help the dog succeed at developing to his fullest potential. Unfortunately, many owners of untrained adult dogs lack the patience factor, so they do

Your Griffon should be taken on a lead to the area in which you prefer for the use of the dog's relief. Be consistent and take it to the same area all the time.

THE HAND THAT FEEDS
To a dog's way of thinking, your hands are like his mouth in terms of a defence mechanism. If you squeeze him too tightly, he might just bite you because that would be his normal response. This is not aggressive biting and, although all biting should be discouraged, you need the discipline in learning how to handle your dog.

is like working with a dry sponge in a pool of water. The pup soaks up whatever you show him and constantly looks for more things to do and learn. At this early age, his body is not yet producing hormones, and therein lies the reason for such a high rate of success. Without hormones, he is focused on his owners and not particularly interested in investigating other places, dogs, people, etc. You are his leader: his provider of food, water, shelter and security. He latches onto you and wants to stay close. He will usually follow you from room to room, will not let you out of his sight when you are outdoors with him and will respond in like manner to the people and animals you encounter. If you greet a friend warmly, he will be happy to greet the person as well. If, however, you are hesitant, even anxious, about the approach of a stranger, he will respond accordingly.

THINK BEFORE YOU BARK
Dogs are sensitive to their master's moods and emotions. Use your voice wisely when communicating with your dog. Never raise your voice at your dog unless you are angry and trying to correct him. 'Barking' at your dog can become as meaningless as 'dogspeak' is to you. Think before you bark!

not persist until their dogs are successful at learning particular behaviours.

Training a puppy aged 10 to 16 weeks (20 weeks at the most)

Once the puppy begins to produce hormones, his natural curiosity emerges and he begins to investigate the world around him. It is at this time when you may notice that the untrained dog begins to wander away from you and even ignore your commands to stay close. When this behaviour becomes a problem, the owner has two choices: get rid of the dog or train him. It is strongly urged that you choose the latter option.

There are usually classes within a reasonable distance from the owner's home, but you can also do a lot to train your dog yourself. Sometimes there are classes available but the tuition is too costly. Whatever the circumstances, the solution to the problem of lack of lesson availability lies within the pages of this book.

This chapter is devoted to helping you train your Griffon at

MEALTIME
Mealtime should be a peaceful time for your puppy. Do not put his food and water bowls in a high-traffic area in the house. For example, give him his own little corner of the kitchen where he can eat undisturbed and where he will not be underfoot. Do not allow small children or other family members to disturb the pup when he is eating.

home. If the recommended procedures are followed faithfully, you may expect positive results that will prove rewarding both to you and your dog.

Whether your new charge is a puppy or a mature adult, the methods of teaching and the techniques we use in training basic behaviours are the same. After all, no dog, whether puppy or adult, likes harsh or inhumane methods. All creatures, however, respond favourably to gentle motivational methods and sincere praise and encourage-ment. Now let us get started.

HONOUR AND OBEY
Dogs are the most honourable animals in existence. They consider another species (humans) as their own. They interface with you. You are their leader. Puppies perceive children to be on their level; their actions around small children are different from their behaviour around their adult masters.

TOILET TRAINING
You can train a puppy to relieve itself wherever you choose, but this must be somewhere suitable. You should bear in mind from the outset that when your puppy is old enough to go out in public

PAPER CAPER

Never line your pup's sleeping area with newspaper. Puppy litters are usually raised on newspaper and, once in your home, the puppy will immediately associate newspaper with voiding. Never put newspaper on any floor while housetraining, as this will only confuse the puppy. If you are paper-training him, use paper in his designated relief area ONLY. Finally, restrict water intake after evening meals. Offer a few licks at a time—never let a young puppy gulp water after meals.

places, any canine deposits must be removed at once. You will always have to carry with you a small plastic bag or 'poop-scoop.'

Outdoor training includes such surfaces as grass, soil and cement. Indoor training usually means training your dog to newspaper.

When deciding on the surface and location that you will want your Griffon to use, be sure it is going to be permanent. Training your dog to grass and then changing your mind two months later is extremely difficult for both dog and owner.

Next, choose the command you will use each and every time you want your puppy to void. 'Hurry up' and 'Toilet' are examples of commands commonly used by dog owners.

Get in the habit of giving the puppy your chosen relief command before you take him out. That way, when he becomes an adult, you will be able to determine if he wants to go out when you ask him. A confirmation will be signs of interest,

ATTENTION!

Your dog is actually training you at the same time you are training him. Dogs do things to get attention. They usually repeat whatever succeeds in getting your attention.

CANINE DEVELOPMENT SCHEDULE

It is important to understand how and at what age a puppy develops into adulthood. If you are a puppy owner, consult the following Canine Development Schedule to determine the stage of development your puppy is currently experiencing. This knowledge will help you as you work with the puppy in the weeks and months ahead.

Period	Age	Characteristics
FIRST TO THIRD	BIRTH TO SEVEN WEEKS	Puppy needs food, sleep and warmth, and responds to simple and gentle touching. Needs mother for security and disciplining. Needs littermates for learning and interacting with other dogs. Pup learns to function within a pack and learns pack order of dominance. Begin socialising with adults and children for short periods. Begins to become aware of its environment.
FOURTH	EIGHT TO TWELVE WEEKS	Brain is fully developed. Needs socialising with outside world. Remove from mother and littermates. Needs to change from canine pack to human pack. Human dominance necessary. Fear period occurs between 8 and 12 weeks. Avoid fright and pain.
FIFTH	THIRTEEN TO SIXTEEN WEEKS	Training and formal obedience should begin. Less association with other dogs, more with people, places, situations. Period will pass easily if you remember this is pup's change-to-adolescence time. Be firm and fair. Flight instinct prominent. Permissiveness and over-disciplining can do permanent damage. Praise for good behaviour.
JUVENILE	FOUR TO EIGHT MONTHS	Another fear period about 7 to 8 months of age. It passes quickly, but be cautious of fright and pain. Sexual maturity reached. Dominant traits established. Dog should understand sit, down, come and stay by now.

NOTE: THESE ARE APPROXIMATE TIME FRAMES. ALLOW FOR INDIVIDUAL DIFFERENCES IN PUPPIES.

wagging his tail, watching you intently, going to the door, etc.

Puppy's Needs

Puppy needs to relieve himself after play periods, after each meal, after he has been sleeping and at any time he indicates that he is looking for a place to urinate or defecate.

The urinary and intestinal tract muscles of very young puppies are not fully developed. Therefore, like human babies, puppies need to relieve themselves frequently.

Take your puppy out often—every hour for an eight-week-old, for example, and always immediately after sleeping and eating. The older the puppy, the less often he will need to relieve himself. Finally, as a mature healthy adult, he will require only three to five relief trips per day.

Housing

Since the types of housing and control you provide for your puppy have a direct relationship on the success of housetraining, we consider the various aspects of both before we begin training.

Taking a new puppy home and turning him loose in your house can be compared to turning a child loose in a sports arena and telling the child that the place is all his! The sheer enormity of the place would be

> **COMMAND STANCE**
> Stand up straight and authoritatively when giving your dog commands. Do not issue commands when lying on the floor or lying on your back on the sofa. If you are on your hands and knees when you give a command, your dog will think you are positioning yourself to play.

too much for him to handle.

Instead, offer the puppy clearly defined areas where he can play, sleep, eat and live. A room of the house where the family gathers is the most obvious choice. Puppies are social animals and need to feel a part of the pack right from the start. Hearing your voice, watching you while you are doing things and smelling you nearby are all positive reinforcers that he is now a member of your pack. Usually a family room, the kitchen or a nearby adjoining breakfast area is ideal for providing safety and security for both puppy and owner.

Within that room there should be a smaller area that the puppy can call his own. An alcove, a wire or fibreglass dog crate or a fenced (not boarded!) corner from which he can view the activities of his new family will be fine. The size of the area or crate is the key factor here.

The area must be large enough for the puppy to lie down and stretch out as well as stand up without rubbing his head on the top, yet small enough so that he cannot relieve himself at one end and sleep at the other without coming into contact with his droppings until fully trained to relieve himself outside.

Dogs are, by nature, clean animals and will not remain close to their relief areas unless forced to do so. In those cases, they then become dirty dogs and usually remain that way for life.

The designated area should contain clean bedding and a toy. Water must always be available, in a non-spill container.

CONTROL

By control, we mean helping the puppy to create a lifestyle pattern that will be compatible to that of his human pack (YOU!). Just as we guide little children to learn our way of life, we must show the puppy when it is time to play, eat, sleep, exercise and even entertain himself.

Your puppy should always sleep in his crate. He should also learn that, during times of household confusion and excessive human activity such as at breakfast when family members are preparing for the day, he can play by himself in relative safety and comfort in his designated area. Each time you

leave the puppy alone, he should understand exactly where he is to stay. Puppies are chewers. They cannot tell the difference between lamp cords, television wires, shoes, table legs, etc. Chewing into a television wire, for example, can be fatal to the puppy while a shorted wire can start a fire in the house.

If the puppy chews on the arm of the chair when he is alone, you will probably discipline him angrily when you get home. Thus, he makes the association that your coming home means he is going to be punished. (He will not remember

Nothing can douse the curiosity of a Griffon puppy...or that of the family cat. Supervise your Griffon puppy as he acquaints himself with all the members of the family.

chewing the chair and is incapable of making the association of the discipline with his naughty deed.)

Other times of excitement, such as family parties, etc., can be fun for the puppy providing he can view the activities from the security of his designated area. He is not underfoot and he is not being fed all sorts of titbits that will probably cause him stomach distress, yet he still feels a part of the fun.

THE SUCCESS METHOD

Success that comes by luck is usually short lived. Success that comes by well-thought-out proven methods is often more easily achieved and permanent. This is the Success Method. It is designed to give you, the puppy owner, a simple yet proven way to help your puppy develop clean living habits and a feeling of security in his new environment.

THE SUCCESS METHOD

1 Tell the puppy 'Crate time!' and place him in the crate with a small treat (a piece of cheese or half of a biscuit). Let him stay in the crate for five minutes while you are in the same room. Then release him and praise lavishly. Never release him when he is fussing. Wait until he is quiet before you let him out.

2 Repeat Step 1 several times a day.

3 The next day, place the puppy in the crate as before. Let him stay there for ten minutes. Do this several times.

4 Continue building time in five-minute increments until the puppy stays in his crate for 30 minutes with you in the room. Always take him to his relief area after prolonged periods in his crate.

5 Now go back to Step 1 and let the puppy stay in his crate for five minutes, this time while you are out of the room.

6 Once again, build crate time in five-minute increments with you out of the room. When the puppy will stay willingly in his crate (he may even fall asleep!) for 30 minutes with you out of the room, he will be ready to stay in it for several hours at a time.

6 Steps to Successful Crate Training

SCHEDULE

A puppy should be taken to his relief area each time he is released from his designated area, after meals, after a play session and when he first awakens in the morning (at age eight weeks, this can mean 5 a.m.!). The puppy will indicate that he's ready 'to go' by circling or sniffing busily—do not misinterpret these signs. For a puppy less than ten weeks of age, a routine of taking him out every hour is necessary. As the puppy grows, he will be able to wait for longer periods of time.

Keep trips to his relief area short. Stay no more than five or six minutes and then return to the house. If he goes during that time, praise him lavishly and take him indoors immediately. If he does not, but he has an accident when you go back indoors, pick him up immediately, say 'No! No!' and return to his relief area. Wait a few minutes, then return to the house again. Never hit a puppy or rub his face in urine or excrement when he has had an accident!

Once indoors, put the puppy in his crate until you have had time to clean up his accident. Then release him to the family area and watch him more closely than before. Chances are, his accident was a result of your not picking up his signal or waiting too long before offering him the opportunity to relieve himself. Never hold a grudge against the puppy for accidents.

Let the puppy learn that going outdoors means it is time to relieve himself, not play. Once trained, he will be able to play

HOW MANY TIMES A DAY?

AGE	RELIEF TRIPS
To 14 weeks	10
14–22 weeks	8
22–32 weeks	6
Adulthood (dog stops growing)	4

These are estimates, of course, but they are a guide to the MINIMUM opportunities a dog should have each day to relieve itself.

'NO' MEANS 'NO!'

Dogs do not understand our language. They can be trained to react to a certain sound, at a certain volume. If you say 'No, Oliver' in a very soft pleasant voice it will not have the same meaning as 'No, Oliver!!' when you shout it as loud as you can. You should never use the dog's name during a reprimand, just the command NO!! Since dogs don't understand words, comics often use dogs trained with opposite meanings. Thus, when the comic commands his dog to SIT the dog will stand up, and vice versa.

indoors and out and still differentiate between the times for play versus the times for relief.

Help him develop regular hours for naps, being alone, playing by himself and just resting, all in his crate. Encourage him to entertain himself while you are busy with your activities. Let him learn that having you near is comforting, but it is not your main purpose in life to provide him with undivided attention.

Each time you put a puppy in his own area, use the same command, whatever suits best. Soon he will run to his crate or special area when he hears you say those words.

Crate training provides safety for you, the puppy and the home. It also provides the puppy with a feeling of security, and that helps the puppy achieve self-confidence and clean habits.

Remember that one of the primary ingredients in housetraining your puppy is control. Regardless of your lifestyle, there will always be occasions when you will need to have a place where your dog can stay and be happy and safe. Crate training is the answer for now and in the future.

In conclusion, a few key elements are really all you need for a successful housetraining method—consistency, frequency, praise, control and supervision. By following these procedures with a normal, healthy puppy, you and the puppy will soon be past the stage of 'accidents' and ready to move on to a full and rewarding life together.

TRAINING RULES

If you want to be successful in training your dog, you have four rules to obey yourself:
1. Develop an understanding of how a dog thinks.
2. Do not blame the dog for lack of communication.
3. Define your dog's personality and act accordingly.
4. Have patience and be consistent.

THE GOLDEN RULE

The golden rule of dog training is simple. For each 'question' (command), there is only one correct answer (reaction). One command = one reaction. Keep practising the command until the dog reacts correctly without hesitating. Be repetitive but not monotonous. Dogs get bored just as people do!

ROLES OF DISCIPLINE, REWARD AND PUNISHMENT

Discipline, training one to act in accordance with rules, brings order to life. It is as simple as that. Without discipline, particularly in a group society, chaos reigns supreme and the group will eventually perish. Humans and canines are social animals and need some form of discipline in order to function effectively. They must procure food, protect their home base and their young and reproduce to keep the species going.

If there were no discipline in the lives of social animals, they would eventually die from starvation and/or predation by other stronger animals.

In the case of domestic canines, dogs need discipline in their lives in order to understand how their pack (you and other family members) functions and how they must act in order to survive.

A large humane society in a highly populated area recently surveyed dog owners regarding their satisfaction with their

TRAINING TIP

Dogs will do anything for your attention. If you reward the dog when he is calm and resting, you will develop a well-mannered dog. If, on the other hand, you greet your dog excitedly and encourage him to wrestle with you, the dog will greet you the same way and you will have a hyperactive dog on your hands.

relationships with their dogs. People who had trained their dogs were 75% more satisfied with their pets than those who had never trained their dogs.

Dr Edward Thorndike, a psychologist, established *Thorndike's Theory of Learning*, which states that a behaviour that results in a pleasant event tends to be repeated. A behaviour that results in an unpleasant event tends not to be repeated. It is this theory on which training methods are based today. For example, if you manipulate a dog to perform a specific behaviour and reward him for doing it, he is likely to do it again because he enjoyed the end result.

Occasionally, punishment, a penalty inflicted for an offence, is necessary. The best type of punishment often comes from an outside source. For example, a child is told not to touch the stove because he may get burned. He disobeys and touches the stove. In doing so, he receives a burn. From that time on, he respects the heat of the stove and avoids contact with it. Therefore, a behaviour that results in an unpleasant event tends not to be repeated.

A good example of a dog learning the hard way is the dog who chases the house cat. He is told many times to leave the cat alone, yet he persists in teasing the cat. Then, one day he begins chasing the cat but the cat turns and swipes a claw across the dog's face, leaving him with a

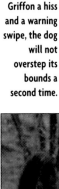
Once the cat has given the Griffon a hiss and a warning swipe, the dog will not overstep its bounds a second time.

painful gash on his nose. The final result is that the dog stops chasing the cat.

TRAINING EQUIPMENT

COLLAR AND LEAD

For a Griffon, the collar and lead that you use for training must be one with which you are easily able to work, not too heavy for the dog and perfectly safe.

TREATS

Have a bag of treats on hand. Something nutritious and easy to swallow works best. Use a soft treat, a chunk of cheese or a piece of cooked chicken rather than a dry biscuit. By the time the dog has finished chewing a dried treat, he will forget why he is being rewarded in the first place! Using food rewards will not teach a dog to beg at the table—the only way to teach a dog to beg at the table is to give him food from the table. In training, rewarding the dog with a food treat will help him associate praise and the treats with learning new behaviours that obviously please his owner.

TRAINING BEGINS: ASK THE DOG A QUESTION

In order to teach your dog anything, you must first get his attention. After all, he cannot learn anything if he is looking away from you with his mind on

The Griffon can be trained to use a 'cat door' to let himself out when he needs to relieve himself. The puppy, however, cannot be trusted to use the 'cat door' until he is completely housetrained.

something else.

To get his attention, ask him, 'School?' and immediately walk over to him and give him a treat as you tell him 'Good dog.' Wait a minute or two and repeat the routine, this time with a treat in your hand as you approach within a foot of the dog. Do not go directly to him, but stop about a foot short of him and hold out the treat as you ask, 'School?' He will see you approaching with a treat in your hand and most likely begin walking toward you. As you meet, give him the treat and praise again.

The third time, ask the question, have a treat in your

hand and walk only a short distance toward the dog so that he must walk almost all the way to you. As he reaches you, give him the treat and praise again.

By this time, the dog will probably be getting the idea that if he pays attention to you, especially when you ask that question, it will pay off in treats and enjoyable activities for him. In other words, he learns that 'school' means doing great things with you that are fun and result in positive attention for him.

Remember that the dog does not understand your verbal language; he only recognises sounds. Your question translates to a series of sounds for him, and those sounds become the signal to go to you and pay attention; if he does, he will get to interact with you plus receive treats and praise.

THE BASIC COMMANDS

TEACHING SIT

Now that you have the dog's attention, attach his lead and hold it in your left hand and a food treat in your right. Place your food hand at the dog's nose and let him lick the treat but not take it from you. Say 'Sit' and slowly raise your food hand from in front of the dog's nose up over his head so that he is looking at the ceiling. As he bends his head upward, he will have to bend his

FEAR AGGRESSION
Pups who are subjected to physical abuse during training commonly end up with behavioural problems as adults. One common result of abuse is fear aggression, in which a dog will lash out, bare his teeth, snarl and finally bite someone by whom he feels threatened. For example, your daughter may be playing with the dog one afternoon. As they play hide-and-seek, she backs the dog into a corner, and as she attempts to tease him playfully, he bites her hand. Examine the cause of this behaviour. Did your daughter ever hit the dog? Did someone who resembles your daughter hit or scream at the dog? Fortunately, fear aggression is relatively easy to correct. Have your daughter engage in only positive activities with the dog, such as feeding, petting and walking. She should not give any corrections or negative feedback. If the dog still growls or cowers away from her, allow someone else to accompany them. After approximately one week, the dog should feel that he can rely on her for many positive things, and he will also be prevented from reacting fearfully towards anyone who might resemble her.

knees to maintain his balance. As he bends his knees, he will assume a sit position. At that point, release the food treat and praise lavishly with comments such as 'Good dog! Good sit!,' etc. Remember to always praise enthusiastically, because dogs relish verbal praise from their owners and feel so proud of themselves whenever they accomplish a behaviour.

You will not use food forever in getting the dog to obey your commands. Food is only used to teach new behaviours, and once the dog knows what you want when you give a specific command, you will wean him off the food treats but still maintain the verbal praise. After all, you

OPEN MINDS
Dogs are as different from each other as people are. What works for one dog may not work for another. Have an open mind. If one method of training is unsuccessful, try another.

will always have your voice with you, and there will be many times when you have no food rewards but expect the dog to obey.

TEACHING DOWN
Teaching the down exercise is easy when you understand how the dog perceives the down position, and it is very difficult when you do not. Dogs perceive the down position as a submissive one, therefore teaching the down exercise using a forceful method can sometimes make the dog develop such a fear of the down that he either runs away when you say 'Down' or he

SAFETY FIRST
While it may seem that the most important things to your dog are eating, sleeping and chewing the upholstery on your furniture, his first concern is actually safety. The domesticated dogs we keep as companions have the same pack instinct as their ancestors who ran free thousands of years ago. Because of this pack instinct, your dog wants to know that he and his pack are not in danger of being harmed, and that his pack has a strong, capable leader. You must establish yourself as the leader early on in your relationship. That way your dog will trust that you will take care of him and the pack, and he will accept your commands without question.

A gaggle of Griffon pups smiling at the camera.

attempts to snap at the person who tries to force him down.

Have the dog sit close alongside your left leg, facing in the same direction as you are. Hold the lead in your left hand and a food treat in your right. Now place your left hand lightly on the top of the dog's shoulders where they meet above the spinal cord. Do not push down on the dog's shoulders; simply rest your left hand there so you can guide the dog to lie down close to your left leg rather than to swing away from your side when he drops.

Now place the food hand at the dog's nose, say 'Down' very softly (almost a whisper), and slowly lower the food hand to the dog's front feet. When the food hand reaches the floor, begin moving it forward along the floor in front of the dog. Keep talking softly to the dog, saying things like, 'Do you want this treat? You can do this, good dog.' Your reassuring tone of voice will help calm the dog as he tries to follow the food hand in order to get the treat.

When the dog's elbows touch the floor, release the food and praise softly. Try to get the dog to maintain that down position for several seconds before you let him sit up again. The goal here is to get the dog to settle down and not feel threatened in the down position.

DOUBLE JEOPARDY
A dog in jeopardy never lies down. He stays alert on his feet because instinct tells him that he may have to run away or fight for his survival. Therefore, if a dog feels threatened or anxious, he will not lie down. Consequently, it is important to have the dog calm and relaxed as he learns the down exercise.

TEACHING STAY

It is easy to teach the dog to stay in either a sit or a down position. Again, we use food and praise during the teaching process as we help the dog to understand exactly what it is that we are expecting him to do.

To teach the sit/stay, start with the dog sitting on your left side as before and hold the lead in your left hand. Have a food treat in your right hand and place your food hand at the dog's nose. Say 'Stay' and step out on your right foot to stand directly in front of the dog, toe to toe, as he licks and nibbles the treat. Be sure to keep his head facing upward to maintain the sit position. Count to five and then swing around to stand next to the dog again with him on your left. As soon as you get back to the original position, release the food and praise lavishly.

To teach the down/stay, do the down as previously described. As soon as the dog lies down, say 'Stay' and step out on your right foot just as you did in the sit/stay. Count to five and then return to stand beside the dog with him on your left side. Release the treat and praise as always.

Within a week or ten days, you can begin to add a bit of distance between you and your dog when you leave him. When you do, use your left hand open with the palm facing the dog as a stay signal, much the same as the hand signal a constable uses to stop traffic at an intersection. Hold the food treat in your right hand as before, but this time the food is not touching the dog's nose. He will watch the food hand and quickly learn that he is going to get that treat as soon as you return to his side.

When you can stand 1 metre away from your dog for 30 seconds, you can then begin building time and distance in both stays. Eventually, the dog

Your Griffon will accept whatever house rules you establish. This Griffon obviously has the run of the house, including climbing on the furniture to enjoy the view of the terrace.

CONSISTENCY PAYS OFF
Dogs need consistency in their feeding schedule, exercise and toilet breaks and in the verbal commands you use. If you use 'Stay' on Monday and 'Stay here, please' on Tuesday, you will confuse your dog. Don't demand perfect behaviour during training classes and then let him have the run of the house the rest of the day. Above all, lavish praise on your pet consistently every time he does something right. The more he feels he is pleasing you, the more willing he will be to learn.

not love the game or that fails to come when called. The secret, it seems, is never to teach the word 'come.'

At times when an owner most wants his dog to come when called, the owner is likely to be upset or anxious and he allows these feelings to come through in the tone of his voice when he calls his dog. Hearing that desperation in his owner's voice, the dog fears the results of going to him and therefore either disobeys outright or runs in the opposite direction. The secret, therefore, is to teach the dog a game and, when you want him to come to you, simply play the game. It is practically a no-fail solution!

To begin, have several members of your family take a few food treats and each go into a different room in the house. Take turns calling the dog, and each person should celebrate the dog's finding him with a treat and lots

can be expected to remain in the stay position for prolonged periods of time until you return to him or call him to you. Always praise lavishly when he stays.

TEACHING COME
If you make teaching 'come' an exciting experience, you should never have a 'student' that does

'COME' . . . BACK
Never call your dog to come to you for a correction or scold him when he reaches you. That is the quickest way to turn a 'Come' command into 'Go away fast!' Dogs think only in the present tense, and your dog will connect the scolding with coming to you, not with the misbehaviour of a few moments earlier.

of happy praise. When a person calls the dog, he is actually inviting the dog to find him and get a treat as a reward for 'winning.'

A few turns of the 'Where are you?' game and the dog will understand that everyone is playing the game and that each person has a big celebration awaiting his success at locating them. Once he learns to love the game, simply calling out 'Where are you?' will bring him running from wherever he is when he hears that all-important question.

The come command is recognised as one of the most important things to teach a dog, but there are trainers who work with thousands of dogs and never teach the actual word 'Come.' Yet these dogs will race to respond to a person who uses the dog's name followed by 'Where are you?' For example, a woman has a 12-year-old companion dog who went blind, but who never fails to locate her owner when asked, 'Where are you?'

Children, in particular, love to play this game with their dogs. Children can hide in smaller places like a shower or bath, behind a bed or under a table. The dog needs to work a little bit harder to find these hiding places, but when he does he loves to celebrate with a treat and a tussle with a favourite youngster.

'WHERE ARE YOU?'

When calling the dog, do not say 'Come.' Say things like, 'Rover, where are you? See if you can find me! I have a biscuit for you!' Keep up a constant line of chatter with coaxing sounds and frequent questions such as, 'Where are you?' The dog will learn to follow the sound of your voice to locate you and receive his reward.

TEACHING HEEL

Heeling means that the dog walks beside the owner without pulling. It takes time and patience on the owner's part to

Show dogs must be trained to heel so that the handler can properly gait the dog for the judge.

succeed at teaching the dog that he (the owner) will not proceed unless the dog is walking calmly beside him. Pulling out ahead on the lead is definitely not acceptable.

Begin by holding the lead in your left hand as the dog sits beside your left leg. Move the loop end of the lead to your right hand but keep your left hand short on the lead so it keeps the dog in close next to you.

Say 'Heel' and step forward on your left foot. Keep the dog close to you and take three steps. Stop and have the dog sit next to you in what we now call the 'heel position.' Praise verbally, but do not touch the dog. Hesitate a moment and begin again with 'Heel,' taking three steps and stopping, at which point the dog is told to sit again.

Your goal here is to have the dog walk those three steps without pulling on the lead. Once he will walk calmly beside you for three steps without pulling, increase the number of steps you take to five. When he will walk politely beside you while you take five steps, you can increase the length of your walk to ten steps. Keep increasing the length of your stroll until the dog will walk quietly beside you without pulling as long as you want him to heel. When you stop heeling, indicate to the dog that the exercise is over by verbally praising as you pet him and say 'OK, good dog.' The 'OK' is used

KEEP SMILING
Never train your dog, puppy or adult, when you are angry or in a sour mood. Dogs are very sensitive to human feelings, especially anger, and if your dog senses that you are angry or upset, he will connect your anger with his training and learn to resent or fear his training sessions.

TUG OF WALK?
If you begin teaching the heel by taking long walks and letting the dog pull you along, he misinterprets this action as an acceptable form of taking a walk. When you pull back on the lead to counteract his pulling, he reads that tug as a signal to pull even harder!

as a release word meaning that the exercise is finished and the dog is free to relax.

If you are dealing with a dog who insists on pulling you around, simply 'put on your brakes' and stand your ground until the dog realises that the two of you are not going anywhere until he is beside you and moving at your pace, not his. It may take some time just standing there to convince the dog that you are the leader and you will be the one to decide on the direction and speed of your travel.

Each time the dog looks up at you or slows down to give a slack lead between the two of you, quietly praise him and say, 'Good heel. Good dog.' Eventually, the dog will begin to respond and within a few days he will be walking politely beside you without pulling on the lead. At first, the training sessions should be kept short and very positive;

soon the dog will be able to walk nicely with you for increasingly longer distances. Remember also to give the dog free time and the opportunity to run and play when you have finished heel practice.

WEANING OFF FOOD IN TRAINING
Food is used in training new behaviours. Once the dog understands what behaviour goes with a specific command, it is time to start weaning him off the food treats. At first, give a treat after each exercise. Then, start to give a treat only after every other exercise. Mix up the times when you offer a food reward and the times when you only offer praise so that the dog will never know when he is going to receive both food and praise and when he is going to receive only praise. This is called a variable ratio reward system and it proves successful because there is always the chance that the owner will produce a treat, so the dog never stops trying for that reward. No matter what, ALWAYS give verbal praise.

OBEDIENCE CLASSES
It is a good idea to enrol in an obedience class if one is available in your area. If yours is a show dog, ringcraft classes would be more appropriate. Many areas have dog clubs that offer basic obedience training as well as

> **TRAINING TIP**
> If you are walking your dog and he suddenly stops and looks straight into your eyes, ignore him. Pull the leash and lead him into the direction you want to walk.

preparatory classes for obedience competition. There are also local dog trainers who offer similar classes.

At dog shows, dogs can earn titles at various levels of competition. The beginning levels of competition include basic behaviours such as sit, down, heel, etc. The more advanced levels of competition include jumping, retrieving, scent discrimination and signal work. The advanced levels require a dog and owner to put a lot of time and effort into their training and the titles that can be earned at these levels of competition are very prestigious.

OTHER ACTIVITIES FOR LIFE
Whether a dog is trained in the structured environment of a class or alone with his owner at home, there are many activities that can bring fun and rewards to both owner and dog once they have mastered basic control.

Teaching the dog to help out around the home, in the garden or on the farm provides great satisfaction to both dog and

owner. In addition, the dog's help makes life a little easier for his owner and raises his stature as a valued companion to his family. It helps give the dog a purpose by occupying his mind and providing an outlet for his energy.

If you are interested in participating in organised competition with your Griffon, there are

activities other than obedience in which you and your dog can become involved. Agility is a popular sport where dogs run through an obstacle course that includes various jumps, tunnels and other exercises to test the dog's speed and co-ordination. Mini-agility has been devised by The Kennel Club for small breeds to participate. The events are essentially the same except all obstacles have been reduced in size. The owners run beside their dogs to give commands and to guide them through the course. Although competitive, the focus is on fun—it's fun to do, fun to watch and great exercise. The Griffon is a particularly good jumper and impressively clears the jumps with ease.

Mini-agility is an excellent outing for the active Griffon. In mini-agility, the obstacles have been reduced in size so that the dogs can participate. The Griffon naturally excels in agility.

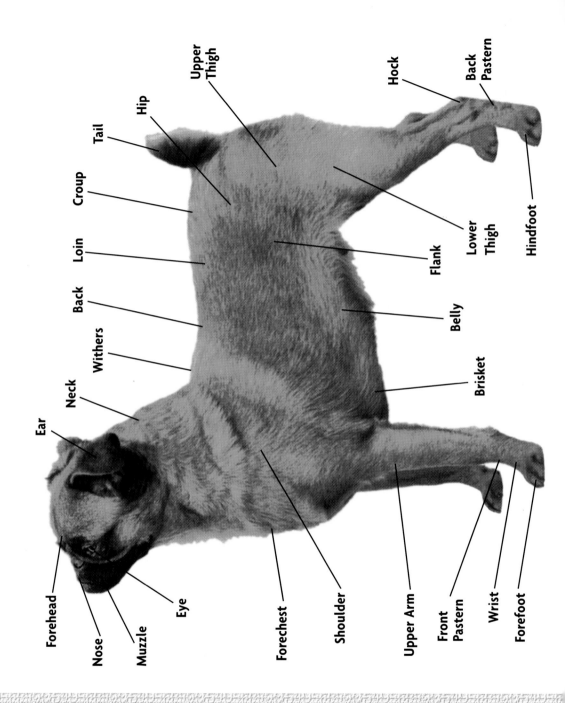

Upper Thigh

Hock

Back Pastern

Hip

Tail

Croup

Loin

Back

Withers

Neck

Ear

Forehead

Nose

Muzzle

Eye

Forechest

Shoulder

Upper Arm

Front Pastern

Wrist

Forefoot

Brisket

Belly

Flank

Lower Thigh

Hindfoot

PHYSICAL STRUCTURE OF THE GRIFFON BRUXELLOIS

Dogs suffer from many of the same physical illnesses as people. They might even share many of the same psychological problems. Since people usually know more about human diseases than canine maladies, many of the terms used in this chapter will be familiar but not necessarily those used by veterinary surgeons. We will use the term *x-ray*, instead of the more acceptable term *radiograph*. We will also use the familiar term *symptoms* even though dogs don't have symptoms, which are verbal descriptions of the patient's feelings; dogs have *clinical signs*. Since dogs can't speak, we have to look for clinical signs...but we still use the term *symptoms* in this book.

As a general rule, medicine is *practised*. That term is not arbitrary. Medicine is a constantly changing art as we learn more and more about genetics, electronic aids (like CAT scans) and daily laboratory advances. There are many dog maladies, like canine hip dysplasia, which are not universally treated in the same manner. Some veterinary surgeons opt for surgery more often than others do.

SELECTING A VETERINARY SURGEON

Your selection of a veterinary surgeon should not be based upon personality (as most are) but upon their convenience to your home. You want a vet who is close because you might have emergencies or need to make multiple visits for treatments. You want a vet who has services that you

A SKUNKY PROBLEM

Have you noticed your dog dragging his rump along the floor? If so, it is likely that his anal sacs are impacted or possibly infected. The anal sacs are small pouches located on both sides of the anus under the skin and muscles. They are about the size and shape of a grape and contain a foul-smelling liquid. Their contents are usually emptied when the dog has a bowel movement, but if they are not emptied completely, they will impact, which will cause your dog a lot of pain. Fortunately, your veterinary surgeon can tend to this problem easily by draining the sacs for the dog. Be aware that your dog might also empty his anal sacs in cases of extreme fright.

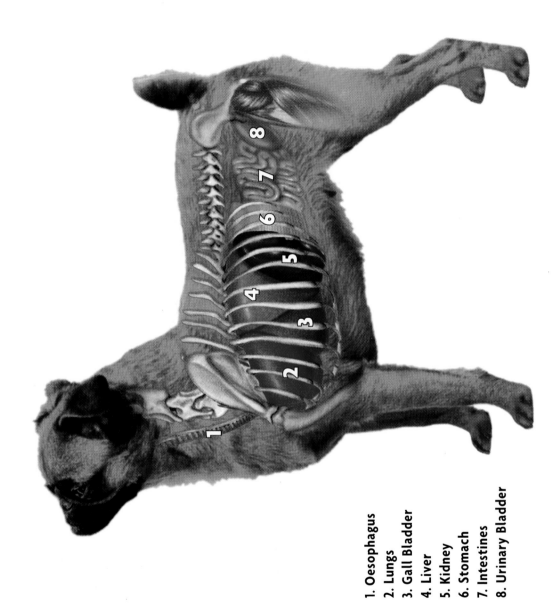

1. Oesophagus
2. Lungs
3. Gall Bladder
4. Liver
5. Kidney
6. Stomach
7. Intestines
8. Urinary Bladder

INTERNAL ORGANS OF THE GRIFFON BRUXELLOIS

might require such as tattooing and grooming, as well as sophisticated pet supplies and a good reputation for ability and responsiveness. There is nothing more frustrating than having to wait a day or more to get a response from your veterinary surgeon.

All veterinary surgeons are licensed and their diplomas and/or certificates should be displayed in their waiting rooms. There are, however, many veterinary specialities that usually require further studies and intern-

Breakdown of Veterinary Income by Category

2%	Dentistry
4%	Radiology
12%	Surgery
15%	Vaccinations
19%	Laboratory
23%	Examinations
25%	Medicines

DISEASE REFERENCE CHART

	What is it?	What causes it?	Symptoms
Leptospirosis	Severe disease that affects the internal organs; can be spread to people.	A bacterium, which is often carried by rodents, that enters through mucous membranes and spreads quickly throughout the body.	Range from fever, vomiting and loss of appetite in less severe cases to shock, irreversible kidney damage and possibly death in most severe cases.
Rabies	Potentially deadly virus that infects warm-blooded mammals. Not seen in United Kingdom.	Bite from a carrier of the virus, mainly wild animals.	1st stage: dog exhibits change in behaviour, fear. 2nd stage: dog's behaviour becomes more aggressive. 3rd stage: loss of coordination, trouble with bodily functions.
Parvovirus	Highly contagious virus, potentially deadly.	Ingestion of the virus, which is usually spread through the faeces of infected dogs.	Most common: severe diarrhoea. Also vomiting, fatigue, lack of appetite.
Kennel cough	Contagious respiratory infection.	Combination of types of bacteria and virus. Most common: *Bordetella bronchiseptica* bacteria and parainfluenza virus.	Chronic cough.
Distemper	Disease primarily affecting respiratory and nervous system.	Virus that is related to the human measles virus.	Mild symptoms such as fever, lack of appetite and mucous secretion progress to evidence of brain damage, 'hard pad.'
Hepatitis	Virus primarily affecting the liver.	Canine adenovirus type I (CAV-1). Enters system when dog breathes in particles.	Lesser symptoms include listlessness, diarrhoea, vomiting. More severe symptoms include 'blue-eye' (clumps of virus in eye).
Coronavirus	Virus resulting in digestive problems.	Virus is spread through infected dog's faeces.	Stomach upset evidenced by lack of appetite, vomiting, diarrhoea.

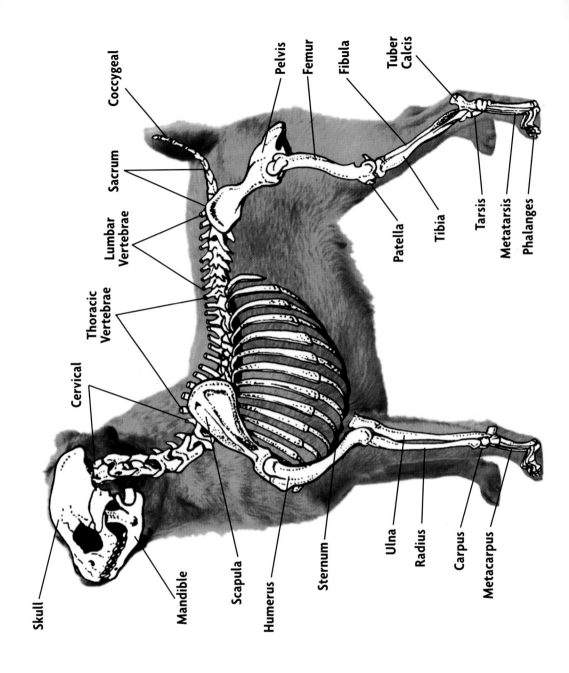

Coccygeal

Pelvis

Femur

Fibula

Tuber Calcis

Sacrum

Tarsis

Metatarsis

Phalanges

Patella

Tibia

Lumbar Vertebrae

Thoracic Vertebrae

Cervical

Skull

Mandible

Scapula

Humerus

Sternum

Ulna

Radius

Carpus

Metacarpus

SKELETAL STRUCTURE OF THE GRIFFON BRUXELLOIS

ships. There are specialists in heart problems (veterinary cardiologists), skin problems (veterinary dermatologists), teeth and gum problems (veterinary dentists), eye problems (veterinary ophthalmologists) and x-rays (veterinary radiologists), as well as vets who have specialities in bones, muscles or other organs. Most veterinary surgeons do routine surgery such as neutering, stitching up wounds and docking tails for those breeds in which such is required for show purposes. When the problem affecting your dog is serious, it is not unusual or impudent to get another medical opinion, although in Britain you are obliged to advise the vets concerned about this. You might also want to compare costs among several veterinary surgeons. Sophisticated health care and veterinary services can be very costly. It is not infrequent that

---

DID YOU KNOW?

Male dogs are neutered. The operation removes the testicles and requires that the dog be anaesthetised. Recovery takes about one week. Females are spayed. This is major surgery and it usually takes a bitch two weeks to recover.

---

important decisions are based upon financial considerations.

PREVENTATIVE MEDICINE

It is much easier, less costly and more effective to practise preventative medicine than to fight bouts of illness and disease. Properly bred puppies come from parents who were selected based upon their genetic disease profile. Their mothers should have been vaccinated, free of all internal and external parasites and properly nourished. For these reasons, a visit to the veterinary surgeon who cared for the dam is recommended. The dam can pass on disease resistance to her puppies, which can last for eight to ten weeks. She can also pass on parasites and many infections. That's why you should visit the veterinary surgeon who cared for the dam.

VACCINATION SCHEDULING

Most vaccinations are given by injection and should only be done by a veterinary surgeon. Both he

---

'P' STANDS FOR PROBLEM

Urinary tract disease is a serious condition that requires immediate medical attention. Symptoms include urinating in inappropriate places or the need to urinate frequently in small amounts. Urinary tract disease is most effectively treated with antibiotics. To help promote good urinary tract health, owners must always be sure that a constant supply of fresh water is available to their pets.

Normal hairs of a dog enlarged 200 times original size. The cuticle (outer covering) is clean and healthy. Unlike human hair that grows from the base, a dog's hair also grows from the end, as shown in the inset. Scanning electron micrographs by Dr Dennis Kunkel, University of Hawaii.

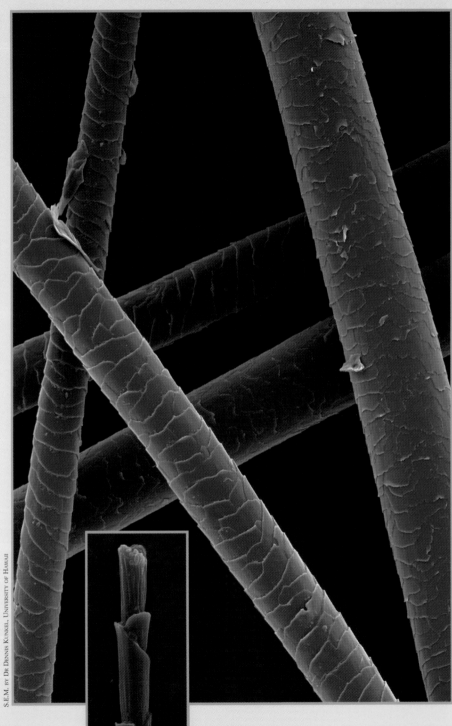

S.E.M. by Dr Dennis Kunkel, University of Hawaii

MORE THAN VACCINES

Vaccinations help prevent your new puppy from contracting diseases, but they do not cure them. Proper nutrition as well as parasite control keep your dog healthy and less susceptible to many dangerous diseases. Remember that your dog depends on you to ensure his well-being.

and you should keep a record of the date of the injection, the identification of the vaccine and the amount given. Some vets give a first vaccination at eight weeks, but most dog breeders prefer the course not to commence until about ten weeks because of negating any antibodies passed on by the dam. The vaccination scheduling is usually based on a 15-day cycle. You must take your vet's advice regarding when to vaccinate as this may differ according to the vaccine used. Most vaccinations immunize your puppy against viruses.

The usual vaccines contain immunizing doses of several different viruses such as

HEALTH AND VACCINATION SCHEDULE

Age in Weeks:	6th	8th	10th	12th	14th	16th	20-24th	1 yr
Worm Control	✔	✔	✔	✔	✔	✔	✔	
Neutering								✔
Heartworm*		✔		✔		✔	✔	
Parvovirus	✔		✔		✔		✔	✔
Distemper		✔		✔		✔		✔
Hepatitis		✔		✔		✔		✔
Leptospirosis								✔
Parainfluenza	✔		✔		✔			✔
Dental Examination		✔					✔	✔
Complete Physical		✔					✔	✔
Coronavirus				✔			✔	✔
Kennel Cough	✔							
Hip Dysplasia								✔
Rabies*							✔	

Vaccinations are not instantly effective. It takes about two weeks for the dog's immune system to develop antibodies. Most vaccinations require annual booster shots. Your veterinary surgeon should guide you in this regard.

*Not applicable in the United Kingdom

distemper, parvovirus, parain-fluenza and hepatitis although some veterinary surgeons recommend separate vaccines for each disease. There are other vaccines available when the puppy is at risk. You should rely upon professional advice. This is especially true for the booster-shot programme. Most vaccination programmes require a booster when the puppy is a year old and once a year thereafter. In some cases, circumstances may require more or less frequent immunizations. Kennel cough, more formally known as tracheobronchitis, is treated with a vaccine that is sprayed into the dog's nostrils. Kennel cough is usually included in routine vaccination, but this is often not so effective as for other major diseases.

WEANING TO FIVE MONTHS OLD

Puppies should be weaned by the time they are about two months old. A puppy that remains for at least eight weeks with its mother and littermates usually adapts better to other dogs and people later in its life.

Some new owners have their puppy examined by a veterinary surgeon immediately, which is a good idea. Vaccination programmes usually begin when the puppy is very young.

The puppy will have its teeth examined and have its skeletal conformation and general health

VACCINE ALLERGIES
Vaccines do not work all the time. Sometimes dogs are allergic to them and many times the antibodies, which are supposed to be stimulated by the vaccine, just are not produced. You should keep your dog in the veterinary clinic for an hour after it is vaccinated to be sure there are no allergic reactions.

checked prior to certification by the veterinary surgeon. Puppies in certain breeds have problems with their kneecaps, cataracts and other eye problems, heart murmurs and undescended testicles. They may also have personality problems and your veterinary surgeon might

KNOW WHEN TO POSTPONE A VACCINATION
While the visit to the vet is costly, it is never advisable to update a vaccination when visiting with a sick or pregnant dog. Vaccinations should be avoided for all elderly dogs. If your dog is showing the signs of any illness or any medical condition, no matter how serious or mild, including skin irritations, do not vaccinate. Likewise, a lame dog should never be vaccinated; any dog undergoing surgery, or a dog on any immunosuppressant drugs should not be vaccinated until fully recovered.

PUPPY VACCINATIONS

Your veterinary surgeon will probably recommend that your puppy be vaccinated before you take him outside. There are airborne diseases, parasite eggs in the grass and unexpected visits from other dogs that might be dangerous to your puppy's health.

have training in temperament evaluation.

FIVE TO TWELVE MONTHS OF AGE

Unless you intend to breed or show your dog, neutering the puppy at six months of age is recommended. Discuss this with your veterinary surgeon. Neutering has proven to be extremely beneficial to both male

Puppies should be weaned from their mother's milk when they are two months old. This dam is looking in on her sleeping brood.

and female puppies. Besides eliminating the possibility of pregnancy, it inhibits (but does not prevent) breast cancer in bitches and prostate cancer in male dogs. Under no circumstances should a bitch be spayed prior to her first season.

Your veterinary surgeon should provide your puppy with a thorough dental evaluation at six months of age, ascertaining whether all the permanent teeth have erupted properly. A home dental care regimen should be initiated at six months, including brushing weekly and providing good dental devices (such as

PARVO FOR THE COURSE
Canine parvovirus is a highly contagious disease that attacks puppies and older dogs. Spread through contact with infected faeces, parvovirus causes bloody diarrhoea, vomiting, heart damage, dehydration, shock and death. To prevent this tragedy, have your puppy begin his series of vaccinations at six to eight weeks. Be aware that the virus is easily spread and is carried on a dog's hair and feet, water bowls and other objects, as well as people's shoes and clothing.

The picture of good health, this Griffon enjoys excellent care from his handsome owner.

Vitamins Recommended for Dogs

Some breeders and vets recommend the supplementation of vitamins to a dog's diet—others do not. Before embarking on a vitamin programme, consult your vet.

Vitamin / Dosage	Food source	Benefits
A / 10,000 IU/week	Eggs, butter, yoghurt, meat	Skin, eyes, hind legs, haircoat
B / Varies	Organs, cottage cheese, sardines	Appetite, fleas, heart, skin and coat
C / 2000 mg+	Fruit, legumes, leafy green vegetables	Healing, arthritis, kidneys
D / Varies	Cod liver, cheese, organs, eggs	Bones, teeth, endocrine system
E / 250 IU daily	Leafy green vegetables, meat, wheat germ oil	Skin, muscles, nerves, healing, digestion
F / Varies	Fish oils, raw meat	Heart, skin, coat, fleas
K / Varies	Naturally in body, not through food	Blood clotting

nylon bones). Regular dental care promotes healthy teeth, fresh breath and a longer life.

ONE TO SEVEN YEARS

Once a year, your grown dog should visit the vet for an examination and vaccination boosters, if needed. Some vets recommend blood tests, thyroid level check and dental evaluation to accompany these annual visits. A thorough clinical evaluation by the vet can provide critical background information for your dog. Blood tests are often performed at one year of age, and dental examinations around the third or fourth birthday. In the long run, quality preventative care for your pet can save money, teeth and lives.

SKIN PROBLEMS IN GRIFFON BRUXELLOIS

Veterinary surgeons are consulted by dog owners for skin problems more than any other group of diseases or maladies. Dogs' skin is almost as sensitive as human skin and both suffer almost the same ailments (though the occurrence

Don't Eat the Daisies!

Many plants and flowers are beautiful to look at, but can be highly toxic if ingested by your dog. Reactions range from abdominal pain and vomiting to convulsions and death. If the following plants are in your home, remove them. If they are outside your house or in your garden, avoid accidents by making sure your dog is never left unsupervised in those locations.

Azalea
Belladonna
Bird of Paradise
Bulbs
Calla lily
Cardinal flower
Castor bean
Chinaberry tree
Daphne

Dumb cane
Dutchman's breeches
Elephant's ear
Hydrangea
Jack-in-the-pulpit
Jasmine
Jimsonweed
Larkspur
Laurel
Lily of the valley

Mescal bean
Mushrooms
Nightshade
Philodendron
Poinsettia
Prunus species
Tobacco
Yellow jasmine
Yews, Taxus species

of acne in dogs is rare!). For this reason, veterinary dermatology has developed into a speciality practised by many veterinary surgeons.

Since many skin problems have visual symptoms that are almost identical, it requires the skill of an experienced veterinary dermatologist to identify and cure many of the more severe skin disorders. Pet shops sell many treatments for skin problems but most of the treatments are directed at symptoms and not the underlying problem(s). If your dog is suffering from a skin disorder, you should seek professional assistance as quickly as possible.

As with all diseases, the earlier a problem is identified and treated, the more successful is the cure.

HEREDITARY SKIN DISORDERS

Veterinary dermatologists are currently researching a number of skin disorders that are believed to have an hereditary basis. These inherited diseases are transmitted

CUSHING'S DISEASE

Cases of hyperactive adrenal glands (Cushing's disease) have been traced to the drinking of highly chlorinated water. Aerate or age your dog's drinking water before offering it.

FACT OR FICTION?
The myth that dogs need extra fat in their diets can be harmful. Should your vet recommend extra fat, use safflower oil instead of animal oils. Safflower oil has been shown to be less likely to cause allergic reactions.

meaning that they carry, but are not affected by, the disease. These diseases pose serious problems to breeders because in some instances there is no method of identifying carriers. Often the secondary diseases associated with these skin conditions are even more debilitating than the disorder itself, including cancers and respiratory problems; others can be lethal.

Among the hereditary skin disorders, for which the mode of

by both parents, who appear (phenotypically) normal but have a recessive gene for the disease,

Fatty Risks
Any dog of any breed can suffer from obesity. Studies show that nearly 30 percent of our dogs are overweight, primarily from high caloric intake and low energy expenditure. The hound and gundog breeds are the most likely affected, and females are at a greater risk of obesity than males. Pet dogs that are neutered are twice as prone to obesity as intact, whole dogs.

Regardless of breed, your dog should have a visible 'waist' behind his rib cage and in front of the hind legs. There should be no fatty deposits on his hips or over his rump, and his abdomen should not be extended.

Veterinary specialists link obesity with respiratory problems, cardiac disease and liver dysfunction as well as low sperm count and abnormal oestrous cycles in breeding animals. Other complications include musculoskeletal disease (including arthritis), decreased immune competence, diabetes mellitus, hypothyroidism, pancreatitis and dermatosis. Other studies have indicated that excess fat leads to heat stress, as obese dogs cannot regulate their body temperatures as well as normal-weight dogs.

Don't be discouraged if you discover that your dog has a heart problem or a complicated neurological condition requiring special attention. It is possible to tend to his special medical needs. Veterinary specialists focus on areas such as cardiology, neurology and oncology. Veterinary medical associations require rigorous training and experience before granting certification in a speciality. Consulting a specialist may offer you greater peace of mind when seeking treatment for your dog.

Discuss heredi-
tary problems
with your chosen
breeder before
selecting a
puppy. Although
hereditary skin
problems are not
known in the
Griffon, other
hereditary
problems are
documented.

inheritance is known, are:
acrodermatitis, cutaneous asthenia
(Ehlers-Danlos syndrome),
sebaceous adenitis, cyclic
hematopoiesis, dermatomyositis,
IgA deficiency, colour dilution
alopecia and nodular dermatofibrosis. Some of these disorders
are limited to one or two breeds
and others affect a large number
of breeds. All inherited diseases
must be diagnosed and treated by
a veterinary specialist.

PARASITE BITES

Many of us are allergic to insect
bites. The bites itch, erupt and
may even become infected. Dogs
have the same reaction to fleas,
ticks and/or mites. When an
insect lands on you, you have the
chance to whisk it away with your
hand. Unfortunately, when your
dog is bitten by a flea, tick or
mite, it can only scratch it away
or bite it. By the time the dog has
been bitten, the parasite has done
some of its damage. It may also
have laid eggs to cause further

problems in the near future. The
itching from parasite bites is
probably due to the saliva injected
into the site when the parasite
sucks the dog's blood.

AUTO-IMMUNE SKIN CONDITIONS

Auto-immune skin conditions are
commonly referred to as being
allergic to yourself, while allergies
are usually inflammatory
reactions to an outside stimulus.
Auto-immune diseases cause
serious damage to the tissues that
are involved.

The best known auto-immune
disease is lupus, which affects
people as well as dogs. The
symptoms are variable and may
affect the kidneys, bones, blood
chemistry and skin. It can be fatal
to both dogs and humans, though
it is not thought to be transmissible. It is usually successfully
treated with cortisone, prednisone
or a similar corticosteroid, but
extensive use of these drugs can
have harmful side effects.

AIRBORNE ALLERGIES

An interesting allergy is pollen
allergy. Humans have hay fever,

> **DID YOU KNOW?**
> Your dog's protein needs are
> changeable. High activity level,
> stress, climate and other physical
> factors may require your dog to
> have more protein in his diet. Check
> with your veterinary surgeon.

PROPER DIET
Feeding your dog properly is very important. An incorrect diet could affect the dog's health, behaviour and nervous system, possibly making a normal dog into an aggressive one.

rose fever and other fevers with which they suffer during the pollinating season. Many dogs suffer from the same allergies. When the pollen count is high, your dog might suffer but don't expect him to sneeze and have a runny nose like a human would. Dogs react to pollen allergies the same way they react to fleas—they scratch and bite themselves.

Dogs, like humans, can be tested for allergens. Discuss the testing with your veterinary dermatologist.

FOOD PROBLEMS

FOOD ALLERGIES

Dogs are allergic to many foods that are best-sellers and highly recommended by breeders and veterinary surgeons. Changing the brand of food that you buy may not eliminate the problem if the element to which the dog is allergic is contained in the new brand.

Recognising a food allergy is difficult. Humans vomit or have rashes when they eat a food to which they are allergic. Dogs neither vomit nor (usually) develop a rash. They react in the same manner as they do to an airborne or flea allergy; they itch, scratch and bite, thus making the diagnosis extremely difficult. While pollen allergies and parasite bites are usually seasonal, food allergies are year-round problems.

FOOD INTOLERANCE

Food intolerance is the inability of the dog to completely digest certain foods. Puppies that may have done very well on their mother's milk may not do well on cow's milk. The result of this food intolerance may be loose bowels, passing gas and stomach pains. These are the only obvious symptoms of food intolerance and that makes diagnosis difficult.

TREATING FOOD PROBLEMS

It is possible to handle food allergies and food intolerance yourself. Put your dog on a diet

The breeder introduces the puppies to solid foods around the fourth or fifth week. Find out what food the pups have been eating before you take your puppy home.

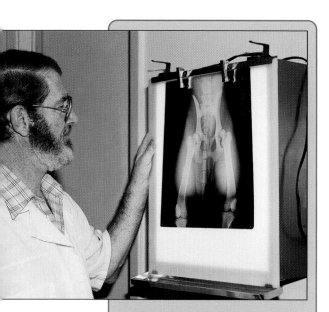

DYSPLASIA CAN BE CORRECTED
Any dog can be born with
dysplastic problems. Your vet can
usually diagnose the potential or
actual problem using x-rays. If
caught early enough, dysplasia
can be corrected.

your dog has a food allergy.

Don't think that the single
ingredient cured the problem. You
still must find a suitable diet and
ascertain which ingredient in the
old diet was objectionable. This is
most easily done by adding
ingredients to the new diet one at
a time. Let the dog stay on the
modified diet for a month before
you add another ingredient.
Eventually, you will determine
the ingredient that caused the
adverse reaction.

MANY KINDS OF EARS
Not every dog's ears are the
same. Ears that are open to the
air are healthier than ears with
poor air circulation. Sometimes a
dog can have two differently
shaped ears. You should not
probe inside your dog's ears. Only
clean that which is accessible
with a soft cotton wipe.

that it has never had. Obviously if
it has never eaten this new food it
can't have been allergic or
intolerant of it. Start with a single
ingredient that is not in the dog's
diet at the present time. Ingredients like chopped beef or fish are
common in dogs' diets, so try
something more exotic like rabbit,
pheasant or even just vegetables.
Keep the dog on this diet (with no
additives) for a month. If the
symptoms of food allergy or
intolerance disappear, chances are

THE SAME ALLERGIES

Chances are that you and your dog will have the same allergies. Your allergies are readily recognisable and usually easily treated. Your dog's allergies may be masked.

DENTAL HEALTH

A dental examination is in order when the dog is between six months and one year of age so any permanent teeth that have erupted incorrectly can be corrected. It is important to begin a brushing routine, preferably using a two-sided brushing technique, whereby both sides of the tooth are brushed at the same time. Durable nylon and safe edible chews should be a part of your puppy's arsenal for good health, good teeth and pleasant breath. The vast majority of dogs three to four years old and older have diseases of the gums from lack of dental attention. Using the various types of dental chews can be very effective in controlling dental plaque.

An alternative method is to carefully study the ingredients in the diet to which your dog is allergic or intolerant. Identify the main ingredient in this diet and eliminate the main ingredient by buying a different food that does not have that ingredient. Keep experimenting until the symptoms disappear after one month on the new diet.

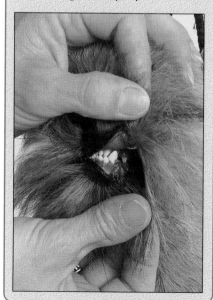

CARETAKER OF TEETH

You are your dog's caretaker and his dentist. Vets warn that plaque and tartar buildup on the teeth will damage the gums and allow bacteria to enter the dog's bloodstream, causing serious damage to the animal's vital organs. Studies show that over 50 percent of dogs have some form of gum disease before age three. Daily or weekly tooth cleaning (with a brush or soft gauze pad wipes) can add years to your dog's life.

EXTERNAL PARASITES

FLEAS

Of all the problems to which dogs are prone, none is more well known and frustrating than fleas. Flea infestation is relatively simple to cure but difficult to prevent. Parasites that are harboured inside the body are a bit more difficult to eradicate but they are easier to control.

To control flea infestation, you have to understand the flea's life cycle. Fleas are often thought of as a summertime problem, but centrally heated homes have changed the patterns and fleas can be found at any time of the year. The most effective method of flea control is a two-stage approach: one stage to kill the adult fleas, and the other to control the development of pre-adult fleas. Unfortunately, no single active ingredient is effective against all stages of the life cycle.

LIFE CYCLE STAGES

During its life, a flea will pass through four life stages: egg, larva, pupa and adult. The adult stage is the most visible and irritating stage of the flea life cycle, and this is why the majority of flea-control products concentrate on this stage.

A scanning electron micrograph (S. E. M.) of a dog flea, *Ctenocephalides canis.*

S. E. M. BY DR DENNIS KUNKEL, UNIVERSITY OF HAWAII

Magnified head of a dog flea, *Ctenocephalides canis.*

S. E. M. BY DR DENNIS KUNKEL, UNIVERSITY OF HAWAII

A Look at Fleas

Fleas have been around for millions of years and have adapted to changing host animals. They are able to go through a complete life cycle in less than one month or they can extend their lives to almost two years by remaining as pupae or cocoons. They do not need blood or any other food for up to 20 months.

They have been measured as being able to jump 300,000 times and can jump 150 times their length in any direction including straight up. Those are just a few of the reasons why they are so successful in infesting a dog!

The fact is that adult fleas account for only 1% of the total flea population, and the other 99% exist in pre-adult stages, i.e. eggs, larvae and pupae. The pre-adult stages are barely visible to the naked eye.

THE LIFE CYCLE OF THE FLEA

Eggs are laid on the dog, usually in quantities of about 20 or 30, several times a day. The female adult flea must have a blood meal before each egg-laying session. When first laid, the eggs will cling to the dog's fur, as the eggs are still moist. However, they will quickly dry out and fall from the dog, especially if the dog moves around or scratches. Many eggs will fall off in the dog's favourite area or an area in which he spends a lot of time, such as his bed.

Once the eggs fall from the dog onto the carpet or furniture, they will hatch into larvae. This takes from one to ten days. Larvae are not particularly mobile, and will usually travel only a few inches from where they hatch. However, they do have a tendency to move away from light and heavy traffic—under furniture and behind doors are common places to find high quantities of flea larvae.

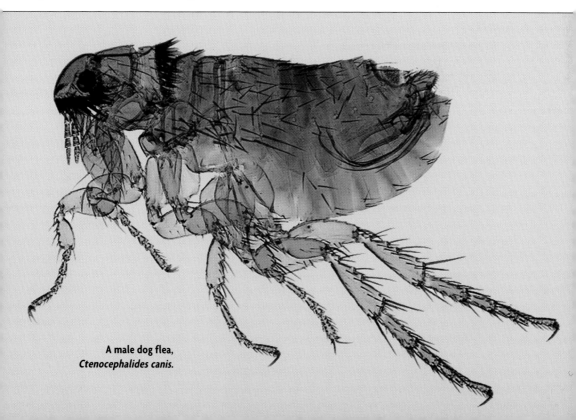

**A male dog flea,
Ctenocephalides canis.**

The flea larvae feed on dead organic matter, including adult flea faeces, until they are ready to change into adult fleas. Fleas will usually remain as larvae for around seven days. After this period, the larvae will pupate into protective pupae. While inside the pupae, the larvae will undergo metamorphosis and change into adult fleas. This can take as little time as a few days, but the adult fleas can remain inside the pupae waiting to hatch for up to two years. The pupae are signalled to hatch by certain stimuli, such as physical pressure—the pupae's being stepped on, heat from an animal lying on the pupae or increased carbon dioxide levels and vibrations—indicating that a suitable host is available.

Once hatched, the adult flea must feed within a few days. Once the adult flea finds a host, it will not leave voluntarily. It only becomes dislodged by grooming or the host animal's scratching. The adult flea will remain on the host for the duration of its life unless forcibly removed.

> **DID YOU KNOW?**
> Never mix flea control products without first consulting your veterinary surgeon. Some products can become toxic when combined with others and can cause serious or fatal consequences.

> **DID YOU KNOW?**
> Flea-killers are poisonous. You should not spray these toxic chemicals on areas of a dog's body that he licks, on his genitals or on his face. Flea killers taken internally are a better answer, but check with your vet in case internal therapy is not advised for your dog.

TREATING THE ENVIRONMENT AND THE DOG

Treating fleas should be a two-pronged attack. First, the environment needs to be treated; this includes carpets and furniture, especially the dog's bedding and areas underneath furniture. The environment should be treated with a household spray containing an Insect Growth Regulator (IGR) and an insecticide to kill the adult fleas. Most IGRs are effective against eggs and larvae; they actually mimic the fleas' own hormones and stop the eggs and larvae from developing into adult fleas. There are currently no treatments available to attack the pupa stage of the life cycle, so the adult insecticide is used to kill the newly hatched adult fleas before they find a host. Most IGRs are active for many months, whilst adult insecticides are only active for a few days.

When treating with a household spray, it is a good idea to vacuum before applying the product. This stimulates as many

Opposite page: A scanning electron micrograph of a dog or cat flea, *Ctenocephalides*, magnified more than 100x. This image has been colorized for effect.

The Life Cycle of the Flea

Eggs

Larva

Pupa

Adult

Photos courtesy of Fleabusters' R₃ for Fleas.

Flea Control

IGR (INSECT GROWTH REGULATOR)

Two types of products should be used when treating fleas—a product to treat the pet and a product to treat the home. Adult fleas represent less than 1% of the flea population. The pre-adult fleas (eggs, larvae and pupae) represent more than 99% of the flea population and are found in the environment; it is in the case of pre-adult fleas that products containing an Insect Growth Regulator (IGR) should be used in the home.

IGRs are a new class of compounds used to prevent the development of insects. They do not kill the insect outright, but instead use the insect's biology against it to stop it from completing its growth. Products that contain methoprene are the world's first and leading IGRs. Used to control fleas and other insects, this type of IGR will stop flea larvae from developing and protect the house for up to seven months.

EN GARDE:
CATCHING FLEAS OFF GUARD!

Consider the following ways to arm yourself against fleas:
• Add a small amount of pennyroyal or eucalyptus oil to your dog's bath. These natural remedies repel fleas.
• Supplement your dog's food with fresh garlic (minced or grated) and a hearty amount of brewer's yeast, both of which ward off fleas.
• Use a flea comb on your dog daily. Submerge fleas in a cup of bleach to kill them quickly.
• Confine the dog to only a few rooms to limit the spread of fleas in the home.
• Vacuum daily...and get all of the crevices! Dispose of the bag every few days until the problem is under control.
• Wash your dog's bedding daily. Cover cushions where your dog sleeps with towels, and wash the towels often.

pupae as possible to hatch into adult fleas. The vacuum cleaner should also be treated with a flea treatment to prevent the eggs and larvae that have been hoovered into the vacuum bag from hatching.

The second stage of treatment is to apply an adult insecticide to the dog. Traditionally, this would be in the form of a collar or a spray, but more recent innovations include digestible insecticides that poison the fleas when they ingest the dog's blood. Alternatively, there are drops that, when placed on the back of the animal's neck, spread throughout the fur and skin to kill adult fleas.

PHOTO BY DWIGHT R KUHN

Dwight R Kuhn's magnificent action photo showing a flea jumping from a dog's back.

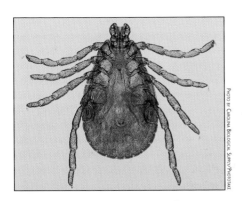

PHOTO BY CAROLINA BIOLOGICAL SUPPLY/PHOTOTAKE

PHOTO BY DR DENNIS KUNKEL, UNIVERSITY OF HAWAII

TICKS AND MITES

Though not as common as fleas, ticks and mites are found all over the tropical and temperate world. They don't bite, like fleas; they harpoon. They dig their sharp proboscis (nose) into the dog's skin and drink the blood. Their only food and drink is dog's blood. Dogs can get Lyme disease, Rocky Mountain spotted fever (normally found in the US only), paralysis and many other diseases from ticks and mites. They may live where fleas are found and they like to hide in cracks or seams in walls wherever dogs live. They are controlled the same way fleas

A brown dog tick, *Rhipicephalus sanguineus*, is an uncommon but annoying tick found on dogs.

The head of a dog tick, *Dermacentor variabilis*, enlarged and coloured for effect.

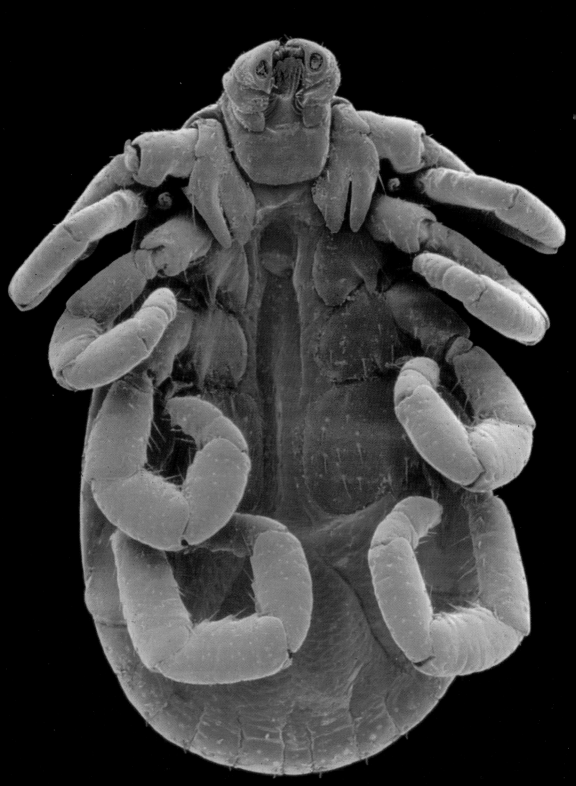

are controlled.

The dog tick, *Dermacentor variabilis*, may well be the most common dog tick in many geographical areas, especially those areas where the climate is hot and humid.

Most dog ticks have life expectancies of a week to six months, depending upon climatic conditions. They can neither jump nor fly, but they can crawl slowly and can range up to 5 metres (16 feet) to reach a sleeping or unsuspecting dog.

BEWARE THE DEER TICK

The great outdoors may be fun for your dog, but it also is a home to dangerous ticks. Deer ticks carry a bacterium known as *Borrelia burgdorferi* and are most active in the autumn and spring. When infections are caught early, penicillin and tetracycline are effective antibiotics, but if left untreated the bacteria may cause neurological, kidney and cardiac problems as well as long-term trouble with walking and painful joints.

Opposite page: The dog tick, *Dermacentor variabilis*, is probably the most common tick found on dogs. Look at the strength in its eight legs! No wonder it's hard to detach them.

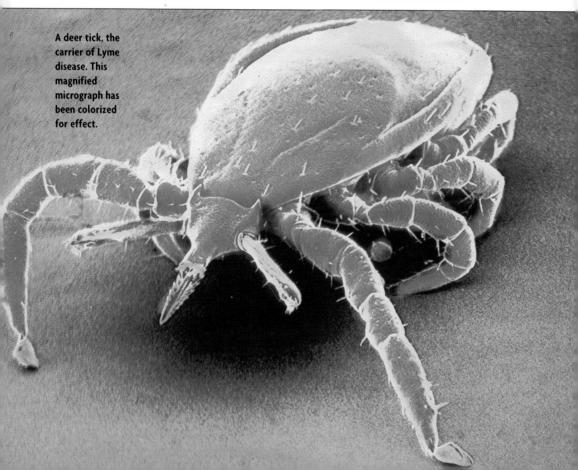

A deer tick, the carrier of Lyme disease. This magnified micrograph has been colorized for effect.

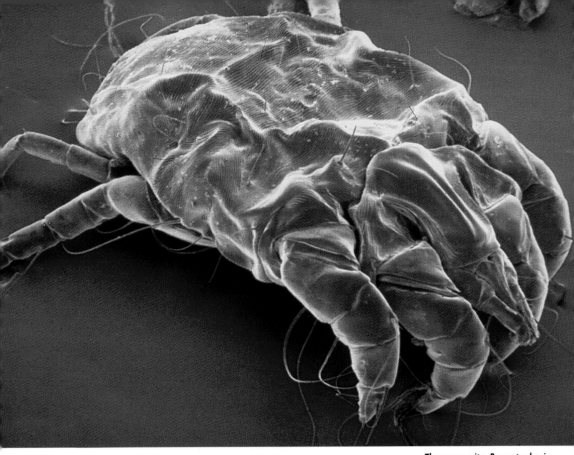

The mange mite, *Psoroptes bovis*.

PHOTO BY DWIGHT R KUHN

Human lice look like dog lice; the two are closely related.

MANGE

Mites cause a skin irritation called mange. Some are contagious, like *Cheyletiella*, ear mites, scabies and chiggers. Mites that cause ear-mite infestations are usually controlled with Lindane, which can only be administered by a vet, followed by Tresaderm at home.

It is essential that your dog be treated for mange as quickly as possible because some forms of mange are transmissible to people.

INTERNAL PARASITES

Most animals—fishes, birds and mammals, including dogs and humans—have worms and other parasites that live inside their bodies. According to Dr Herbert R Axelrod, the fish pathologist, there are two kinds of parasites: dumb and smart. The smart parasites live in peaceful cooperation with their hosts (symbiosis), while the dumb parasites kill their hosts. Most of the worm infections are relatively easy to control. If they are not controlled, they weaken the host dog to the point that other medical problems occur, but they are not dumb parasites.

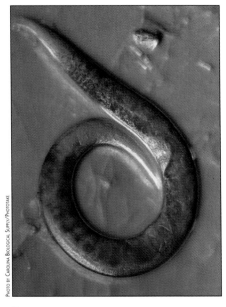

PHOTO BY CAROLINA BIOLOGICAL SUPPLY/PHOTOTAKE

The roundworm, *Rhabditis*. The roundworm can infect both dogs and humans.

ROUNDWORM

Average size dogs can pass 1,360,000 roundworm eggs every day.

For example, if there were only 1 million dogs in the world, the world would be saturated with 1,300 metric tonnes of dog faeces.

These faeces would contain 15,000,000,000 roundworm eggs.

It's known that 7–31% of home gardens and children's play boxes in the US contain roundworm eggs.

Flushing dog's faeces down the toilet is not a safe practice because the usual sewage treatments do not destroy roundworm eggs.

Infected puppies start shedding roundworm eggs at 3 weeks of age. They can be infected by their mother's milk.

ROUNDWORMS

The roundworms that infect dogs are scientifically known as *Toxocara canis*. They live in the dog's intestines. The worms shed eggs continually. It has been estimated that a dog produces about 150 grammes of faeces every day. Each gramme of faeces averages 10,000–12,000 eggs of roundworms. There are no known areas in which dogs roam that do not contain roundworm eggs. The greatest danger of roundworms is that they infect people too! It is wise to have your dog tested regularly for roundworms.

Pigs also have roundworm infections that can be passed to humans and dogs. The typical roundworm parasite is called *Ascaris lumbricoides*.

DEWORMING

Ridding your puppy of worms is VERY IMPORTANT because certain worms that puppies carry, such as tapeworms and roundworms, can infect humans.

Breeders initiate a deworming programme at or about four weeks of age. The routine is repeated every two or three weeks until the puppy is three months old. The breeder from whom you obtained your puppy should provide you with the complete details of the deworming programme.

Your veterinary surgeon can prescribe and monitor the programme of deworming for you. The usual programme is treating the puppy every 15–20 days until the puppy is positively worm-free.

It is advised that you only treat your puppy with drugs that are recommended professionally.

HOOKWORMS

The worm *Ancylostoma caninum* is commonly called the dog hookworm. It is also dangerous to humans and cats. It has teeth by which it attaches itself to the intestines of the dog. It changes the site of its attachment about six times a day and the dog loses blood from each detachment, possibly causing iron-deficiency anaemia. Hookworms are easily purged from the dog with many medications. Milbemycin oxime, which also serves as a heartworm preventative in Collies, can be used for this purpose.

In Britain the 'temperate climate' hookworm (*Uncinaria stenocephala*) is rarely found in pet or show dogs, but can occur in hunting packs, racing Greyhounds and sheepdogs because the worms can be prevalent wherever dogs are exercised regularly on grassland.

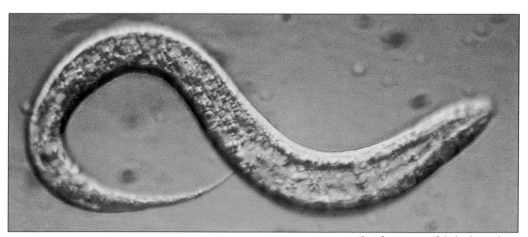

The infective stage of the hookworm larva.

PHOTO BY DWIGHT R KUHN

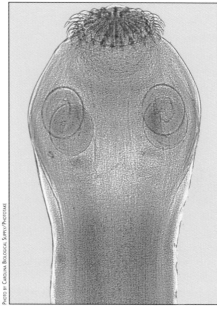

PHOTO BY CAROLINA BIOLOGICAL SUPPLY/PHOTOTAKE

Left:
Male and female hookworms, *Ancylostoma caninum*, are uncommonly found in pet or show dogs in Britain. Hookworms may infect other dogs that have exposure to grasslands.

Right:
The head and rostellum (the round prominence on the scolex) of a tapeworm, which infects dogs and humans.

TAPEWORM

Humans, rats, squirrels, foxes, coyotes, wolves, mixed breeds of dogs and purebred dogs are all susceptible to tapeworm infection. Except in humans, tapeworm is usually not a fatal infection.

Infected individuals can harbour a thousand parasitic worms.

Tapeworms have two sexes—male and female (many other worms have only one sex—male and female in the same worm).

If dogs eat infected rats or mice, they get the tapeworm disease.

One month after attaching to a dog's intestine, the worm starts shedding eggs. These eggs are infective immediately.

Infective eggs can live for a few months without a host animal.

TAPEWORMS

There are many species of tapeworm. They are carried by fleas! The dog eats the flea and starts the tapeworm cycle. Humans can also be infected with tapeworms, so don't eat fleas! Fleas are so small that your dog could pass them onto your hands, your plate or your food and thus make it possible for you to ingest a flea that is carrying tapeworm eggs.

While tapeworm infection is not life-threatening in dogs (smart parasite!), it can be the cause of a very serious liver disease for humans. About 50 percent of the humans infected with *Echinococcus multilocularis*, a type of tapeworm that causes alveolar hydatis, perish.

HEARTWORMS

Heartworms are thin, extended worms up to 30 cms (12 ins) long, which live in a dog's heart and the major blood vessels surrounding it. Dogs may have up to 200 worms. Symptoms may be loss of energy, loss of appetite, coughing, the development of a pot belly and anaemia.

Heartworms are transmitted by mosquitoes. The mosquito drinks the blood of an infected dog and takes in larvae with the blood. The larvae, called microfilaria, develop within the body of the mosquito and are passed on to the next dog bitten after the larvae mature. It takes two to three weeks for the larvae to develop to the infective stage within the body of the mosquito. Dogs should be treated at about six weeks of age, and maintained on a prophylactic dose given monthly.

Blood testing for heartworms is not necessarily indicative of how seriously your dog is infected. This is a dangerous disease. Although heartworm is a problem for dogs in America, Australia, Asia and Central Europe, dogs in the United Kingdom are not currently affected by heartworm.

The heart of a dog infected with canine heartworm, *Dirofilaria immitis.*

PHOTO BY JAMES E HAYDEN, RPB/PHOTOTAKE

First Aid at a Glance

Burns
Place the affected area under cool water; use ice if only a small area is burnt.

Bee/Insect bites
Apply ice to relieve swelling; antihistamine dosed properly.

Animal bites
Clean any bleeding area; apply pressure until bleeding subsides; go to the vet.

Spider bites
Use cold compress and a pressurised pack to inhibit venom's spreading.

Antifreeze poisoning
Induce vomiting with hydrogen peroxide. Seek *immediate* veterinary help!

Fish hooks
Removal best handled by vet; hook must be cut in order to remove.

Snake bites
Pack ice around bite; contact vet quickly; identify snake for proper antivenin.

Car accident
Move dog from roadway with blanket; seek veterinary aid.

Shock
Calm the dog, keep him warm; seek immediate veterinary help.

Nosebleed
Apply cold compress to the nose; apply pressure to any visible abrasion.

Bleeding
Apply pressure above the area; treat wound by applying a cotton pack.

Heat stroke
Submerge dog in cold bath; cool down with fresh air and water; go to the vet.

Frostbite/Hypothermia
Warm the dog with a warm bath, electric blankets or hot water bottles.

Abrasions
Clean the wound and wash out thoroughly with fresh water; apply antiseptic.

 Remember: an injured dog may attempt to bite a helping hand from fear and confusion. Always muzzle the dog before trying to offer assistance.

HOMEOPATHY:
an alternative
to conventional
medicine

'Less is Most'
Using this principle, the strength of a homeopathic remedy is measured by the number of serial dilutions that were undertaken to create it. The greater the number of serial dilutions, the greater the strength of the homeopathic remedy. The potency of a remedy that has been made by making a dilution of 1 part in 100 parts (or 1/100) is 1c or 1cH. If this remedy is subjected to a series of further dilutions, each one being 1/100, a more dilute and stronger remedy is produced. If the remedy is diluted in this way six times, it is called 6c or 6cH. A dilution of 6c is 1 part in 1,000,000,000,000. In general, higher potencies in more frequent doses are better for acute symptoms and lower potencies in more infrequent doses are more useful for chronic, long-standing problems.

CURING OUR DOGS NATURALLY
Holistic medicine means treating the whole animal as a unique, perfect living being. Generally, holistic treatments do not suppress the symptoms that the body naturally produces, as do most medications prescribed by conventional doctors and vets. Holistic methods seek to cure disease by regaining balance and harmony in the patient's environment. Some of these methods include use of nutritional therapy, herbs, flower essences, aromatherapy, acupuncture, massage, chiropractic and, of course the most popular holistic approach, homeopathy. Homeopathy is a theory or system of treating illness with small doses of substances which, if administered in larger quantities, would produce the symptoms that the patient already has. This approach is often described as 'like cures like.' Although modern veterinary medicine is geared toward the 'quick fix,' homeopathy relies on the belief that, given the time, the body is able to heal itself and return to its natural, healthy state.

Choosing a remedy to cure a problem in our dogs is the difficult part of homeopathy. Consult with your veterinary surgeon for a professional diagnosis of your dog's symptoms. Often these symptoms require immediate conventional

care. If your vet is willing, and knowledgeable, you may attempt a homeopathic remedy. Be aware that cortisone prevents homeopathic remedies from working. There are hundreds of possibilities and combinations to cure many problems in dogs, from basic physical problems such as excessive moulting, fleas or other parasites, unattractive doggy odour, bad breath, upset tummy, dry, oily or dull coat, diarrhoea, ear problems or eye discharge (including tears and dry or mucousy matter), to behavioural abnormalities, such as fear of loud noises, habitual licking, poor appetite, excessive barking, obesity and various phobias. From alumina to zincum metallicum, the remedies span the planet and the imagination…from flowers and weeds to chemicals, insect droppings, diesel smoke and volcanic ash.

Using 'Like to Treat Like'

Unlike conventional medicines that suppress symptoms, homeopathic remedies treat illnesses with small doses of substances that, if administered in larger quantities, would produce the symptoms that the patient already has. Whilst the same homeopathic remedy can be used to treat different symptoms in different dogs, here are some interesting remedies and their uses.

Apis Mellifica
(made from honey bee venom) can be used for allergies or to reduce swelling that occurs in acutely infected kidneys.

Diesel Smoke
can be used to help control travel sickness.

Calcarea Fluorica
(made from calcium fluoride which helps harden bone structure) can be useful in treating hard lumps in tissues.

Natrum Muriaticum
(made from common salt, sodium chloride) is useful in treating thin, thirsty dogs.

Nitricum Acidum
(made from nitric acid) is used for symptoms you would expect to see from contact with acids such as lesions, especially where the skin joins the linings of body orifices or openings such as the lips and nostrils.

Symphytum
(made from the herb Knitbone, *Symphytum officianale*) is used to encourage bones to heal.

Urtica Urens
(made from the common stinging nettle) is used in treating painful, irritating rashes.

HOMEOPATHIC REMEDIES FOR YOUR DOG

Symptom/Ailment	Possible Remedy
ALLERGIES	Apis Mellifica 30c, Astacus Fluviatilis 6c, Pulsatilla 30c, Urtica Urens 6c
ALOPECIA	Alumina 30c, Lycopodium 30c, Sepia 30c, Thallium 6c
ANAL GLANDS (BLOCKED)	Hepar Sulphuris Calcareum 30c, Sanicula 6c, Silicea 6c
ARTHRITIS	Rhus Toxicodendron 6c, Bryonia Alba 6c
CATARACT	Calcarea Carbonica 6c, Conium Maculatum 6c, Phosphorus 30c, Silicea 30c
CONSTIPATION	Alumina 6c, Carbo Vegetabilis 30c, Graphites 6c, Nitricum Acidum 30c, Silicea 6c
COUGHING	Aconitum Napellus 6c, Belladonna 30c, Hyoscyamus Niger 30c, Phosphorus 30c
DIARRHOEA	Arsenicum Album 30c, Aconitum Napellus 6c, Chamomilla 30c, Mercurius Corrosivus 30c
DRY EYE	Zincum Metallicum 30c
EAR PROBLEMS	Aconitum Napellus 30c, Belladonna 30c, Hepar Sulphuris 30c, Tellurium 30c, Psorinum 200c
EYE PROBLEMS	Borax 6c, Aconitum Napellus 30c, Graphites 6c, Staphysagria 6c, Thuja Occidentalis 30c
GLAUCOMA	Aconitum Napellus 30c, Apis Mellifica 6c, Phosphorus 30c
HEAT STROKE	Belladonna 30c, Gelsemium Sempervirens 30c, Sulphur 30c
HICCOUGHS	Cinchona Deficinalis 6c
HIP DYSPLASIA	Colocynthis 6c, Rhus Toxicodendron 6c, Bryonia Alba 6c
INCONTINENCE	Argentum Nitricum 6c, Causticum 30c, Conium Maculatum 30c, Pulsatilla 30c, Sepia 30c
INSECT BITES	Apis Mellifica 30c, Cantharis 30c, Hypericum Perforatum 6c, Urtica Urens 30c
ITCHING	Alumina 30c, Arsenicum Album 30c, Carbo Vegetabilis 30c, Hypericum Perforatum 6c, Mezerium 6c, Sulphur 30c
KENNEL COUGH	Drosera 6c, Ipecacuanha 30c
MASTITIS	Apis Mellifica 30c, Belladonna 30c, Urtica Urens 1m
PATELLAR LUXATION	Gelsemium Sempervirens 6c, Rhus Toxicodendron 6c
PENIS PROBLEMS	Aconitum Napellus 30c, Hepar Sulphuris Calcareum 30c, Pulsatilla 30c, Thuja Occidentalis 6c
PUPPY TEETHING	Calcarea Carbonica 6c, Chamomilla 6c, Phytolacca 6c
TRAVEL SICKNESS	Cocculus 6c, Petroleum 6c

Recognising a Sick Dog

Unlike colicky babies and cranky children, our canine kids cannot tell us when they are feeling ill. Therefore, there are a number of signs that owners can identify to know that their dogs are not feeling well.

Take note for physical manifestations such as:

- unusual, bad odour, including bad breath
- excessive moulting
- wax in the ears, chronic ear irritation
- oily, flaky, dull haircoat
- mucous, tearing or similar discharge in the eyes
- fleas or mites
- mucous in stool, diarrhoea
- sensitivity to petting or handling
- licking at paws, scratching face, etc.

Keep an eye out for behavioural changes as well including:

- lethargy, idleness
- lack of patience or general irritability
- lack of appetite, digestive problems
- phobias (fear of people, loud noises, etc.)
- strange behaviour, suspicion, fear
- coprophagia
- more frequent barking
- whimpering, crying

Get Well Soon

You don't need a DVR or a BVMA to provide good TLC to your sick or recovering dog, but you do need to pay attention to some details that normally wouldn't bother him. The following tips will aid Fido's recovery and get him back on his paws again:

- Keep his space free of irritating smells, like heavy perfumes and air fresheners.
- Rest is the best medicine! Avoid harsh lighting that will prevent your dog from sleeping. Shade him from bright sunlight during the day and dim the lights in the evening.
- Keep the noise level down. Animals are more sensitive to sound when they are sick.
- Be attentive to any necessary temperature adjustments. A dog with a fever needs a cool room and cold liquids. A bitch that is whelping or recovering from surgery will be more comfortable in a warm room, consuming warm liquids and food.
- You wouldn't send a sick child back to school early, so don't rush your dog back into a full routine until he seems absolutely ready.

Since the Griffon possesses large eyes, problems are frequently encountered by pet owners.

A PET OWNER'S GUIDE TO COMMON OPHTHALMIC DISEASES
by Prof. Dr Robert L Peiffer, Jr.

Few would argue that vision is the most important of the cognitive senses, and maintenance of a normal visual system is important for an optimal quality of life. Likewise, pet owners tend to be acutely aware of their pet's eyes and vision, which is important because early detection of ocular disease will optimise therapeutic outcomes. The eye is a sensitive organ with minimal reparative capabilities, and with some diseases, such as glaucoma, uveitis and retinal detachment, delay in diagnosis and treatment can be critical in terms of whether vision can be preserved.

Lower entropion, or rolling in of the eyelid, is causing irritation in the left eye of this young dog. Several extra eyelashes, or distichiasis, are present on the upper lid.

The causes of ocular disease are quite varied; the nature of dogs make them susceptible to traumatic conditions, the most common of which include proptosis of the globe, cat scratch injuries and penetrating wounds from foreign objects, including sticks and air rifle pellets. Infectious diseases caused by bacteria, viruses or fungi may be localised to the eye or part of a systemic infection. Many of the common conditions, including eyelid conformational problems, cataracts, glaucoma and retinal degenerations have a genetic basis.

Before acquiring your puppy it is important to ascertain that both parents have been examined and certified free of eye disease by a veterinary ophthalmologist. Since many of these genetic diseases can be detected early in life, acquire the pup with the condition that it pass a thorough ophthalmic examination by a qualified specialist.

LID CONFORMATIONAL ABNORMALITIES
Rolling in (entropion) or out (ectropion) of the lids tends to be a breed-related problem. Entropion can involve the upper and/or lower lids. Signs usually appear between 3 and 12 months of age. The irritation caused by the eyelid hairs rubbing

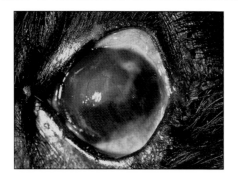

on the surface of the cornea may result in blinking, tearing and damage to the cornea. Ectropion is likewise breed-related and is considered 'normal' in hounds, for instance; unlike entropion, which results in acute discomfort, ectropion may cause chronic irritation related to exposure and the pooling of secretions. Most of these cases can be managed medically with daily irrigation with sterile saline and topical antibiotics when required.

Eyelash Abnormalities
Dogs normally have lashes only on the upper lids, in contrast to humans. Occasionally, extra eyelashes may be seen emerging at the eyelid margin (distichiasis) or through the inner surface of the eyelid (ectopic cilia).

Conjunctivitis
Inflammation of the conjunctiva, the pink tissue that lines the lids and the anterior portion of the sclera, is generally accompanied by redness, discharge and mild discomfort. The majority of cases are either associated with bacterial infections or dry eye syndrome. Fortunately, topical medications are generally effective in curing or controlling the problem.

Dry Eye Syndrome
Dry eye syndrome (keratoconjunctivitis sicca) is a common cause of external ocular disease. Discharge is typically thick and sticky, and keratitis is a frequent component; any breed can be affected. While some cases can be associated with toxic effects of drugs, including the sulfa antibiotics, the cause in the majority of the cases cannot be determined and is assumed to be immune-mediated.

Keratoconjunctivitis sicca, seen here in the right eye of a middle-aged dog, causes a characteristic thick mucous discharge as well as secondary corneal changes.

Left: Prolapse of the gland of the third eyelid in the right eye of a pup. Right: In this case, in the right eye of a young dog, the prolapsed gland can be seen emerging between the edge of the third eyelid and the corneal surface.

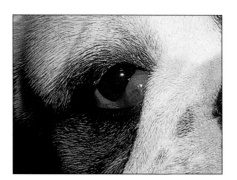

Multiple deep ulcerations affect the cornea of this middle-aged dog.

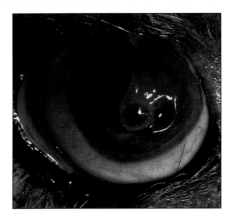

Prolapse of the Gland of the Third Eyelid

In this condition, commonly referred to as *cherry eye*, the gland of the third eyelid, which produces about one-third of the aqueous phase of the tear film and is normally situated within the anterior orbit, prolapses to emerge as a pink fleshy mass protruding over the edge of the third eyelid, between the third eyelid and the cornea. The condition usually develops during the first year of life and, while mild irritation may result, the condition is unsightly as much as anything else.

Lipid deposition can occur as a primary inherited dystrophy, or secondarily to hypercholesterolemia (in dogs frequently associated with hypothyroidism), chronic corneal inflammation or neoplasia. The deposits in this dog assume an oval pattern in the centre of the cornea.

Corneal Disease

The cornea is the clear front part of the eye that provides the first step in the collection of light on its journey to be eventually focused onto the retina, and most corneal diseases will be manifested by alterations in corneal transparency. The cornea is an exquisitely innervated tissue, and defects in corneal integrity are accompanied by pain, which is demonstrated by squinting.

Corneal ulcers may occur secondary to trauma or to irritation from entropion or ectopic cilia. In middle-aged or older dogs, epithelial ulcerations may occur spontaneously due to an inherent defect; these are referred to as indolent or Boxer ulcers, in recognition of the breed in which we see the condition most frequently. Infection may occur secondarily. Ulcers can be potentially blinding conditions; severity is dependent upon the size and depth of the ulcer and other complicating features.

Non-ulcerative keratitis tends to have an immune-mediated component and is managed by topical immunosuppressants, usually corticosteroids. Corneal edema can occur in elderly dogs. It is due to a failure of the corneal endothelial 'pump.'

The cornea responds to chronic irritation by transforming

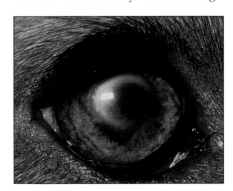

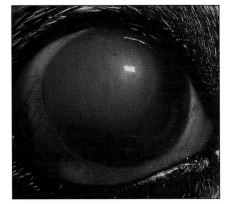

into skin-like tissue that is evident clinically by pigmentation, scarring and vascularisation; some cases may respond to tear stimulants, lubricants and topical corticosteroids, while others benefit from surgical narrowing of the eyelid opening in order to enhance corneal protection.

Uveitis

Inflammation of the vascular tissue of the eye—the uvea—is a common and potentially serious disease in dogs. While it may occur secondarily to trauma or other intraocular diseases, such as

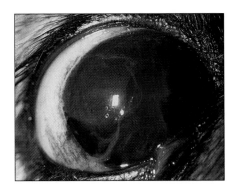

cataracts, most commonly uveitis is associated with some type of systemic infectious or neoplastic process. Uncontrolled, uveitis can lead to blinding cataracts, glaucoma and/or retinal detachments, and aggressive symptomatic therapy with dilating agents (to prevent pupillary adhesions) and anti-inflammatories are critical.

Glaucoma

The eye is essentially a hollow fluid-filled sphere, and the pressure within is maintained by regulation of the rate of fluid production and fluid egress at 10–20 mms of mercury. The retinal cells are extremely sensitive to elevations of intraocular pressure and, unless controlled, permanent blindness can occur within hours to days. In acute glaucoma, the conjunctiva becomes congested, the cornea cloudy, the pupil moderate and fixed; the eye is generally painful and avisual. Increased constant signs of

Corneal edema can develop as a slowly progressive process in elderly Boston Terriers, Miniature Dachshunds and Miniature Poodles, as well as others, as a result of the inability of the corneal endothelial 'pump' to maintain a state of dehydration.

Medial pigmentary keratitis in this dog is associated with irritation from prominent facial folds.

Glaucoma in the dog most commonly occurs as a sudden extreme elevation of intraocular pressure, frequently to three to four times the norm. The eye of this dog demonstrates the common signs of episcleral injection, or redness; mild diffuse corneal cloudiness, due to edema; and a mid-sized fixed pupil.

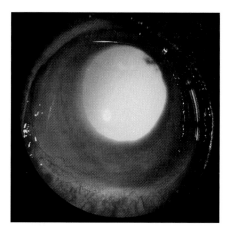

discomfort will accompany chronic cases.

Management of glaucoma is one of the most challenging situations the veterinary ophthalmologist faces; in spite of intense efforts, many of these cases will result in blindness.

CATARACTS AND LENS DISLOCATION

Cataracts are the most common blinding condition in dogs; fortunately, they are readily amenable to surgical intervention, with excellent results in terms of restoration of vision and replace-

ment of the cataractous lens with a synthetic one. Most cataracts in dogs are inherited; less commonly cataracts can be secondary to trauma, other ocular diseases, including uveitis, glaucoma, lens luxation and retinal degeneration, or secondary to an underlying systemic metabolic disease, including diabetes and Cushing's disease. Signs include a progressive loss of the bright dark appearance of the pupil, which is replaced by a blue-grey hazy appearance. In this respect, cataracts need to be distinguished from the normal ageing process of nuclear sclerosis, which occurs in middle-aged or older animals, and has minimal effect on vision.

Lens dislocation occurs in dogs and frequently leads to secondary glaucoma; early removal of the dislocated lens is generally curative.

RETINAL DISEASE

Retinal degenerations are usually inherited, but may be associated with vitamin E deficiency in dogs.

Left: The typical posterior subcapsular cataract appears between one and two years of age, but rarely progresses to where the animal has visual problems. Right: Inherited cataracts generally appear between three and six years of age, and progress to the stage seen where functional vision is significantly impaired.

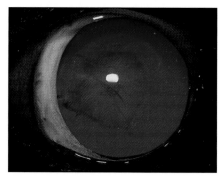

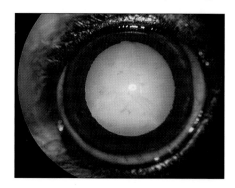

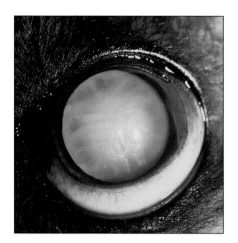

While signs are variable, most frequently one notes a decrease in vision over a period of months, which typically starts out as a night blindness. The cause of a more rapid loss of vision due to retinal degeneration occurs over days to weeks is labeled sudden acquired retinal degeneration or SARD; the outcome, however, is unfortunately usually similar to inherited and nutritional conditions, as the retinal tissues possess minimal regenerative capabilities. Most pets, however, with a bit of extra care and attention, show an amazing ability to adapt to an avisual world, and can be maintained as pets with a satisfactory quality of life. Detachment of the retina—due to accumulation of blood between the retina and the underling uvea, which is called the *choroid*—can occur secondarily to retinal tears or holes, tractional forces within the eye, or as a result of uveitis. These types of detachments may be amenable to surgical repair if diagnosed early.

OPTIC NERVE

Optic neuritis, or inflammation of the nerve that connects the eye with the brain stem, is a relatively uncommon condition that presents usually with rather sudden loss of vision and widely dilated non-responsive pupils.

Anterior lens luxation can occur as a primary disease in the terrier breeds, or secondarily to trauma. The fibres that hold the lens in place rupture and the lens may migrate through the pupil to be situated in front of the iris. Secondary glaucoma is a frequent and significant complication that can be avoided if the dislocated lens is removed surgically.

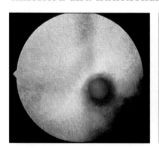
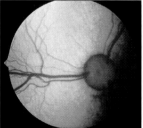
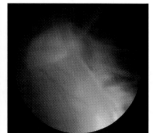

Left: The posterior pole of a normal fundus is shown; prominent are the head of the optic nerve and the retinal blood vessels. The retina is transparent, and the prominent green tapetum is seen superiorly.
Centre: An eye with inherited retinal dysplasia is depicted. The tapetal retina superior to the optic disc is disorganised, with multifocal areas of hyperplasia of the retinal pigment epithelium.
Right: Severe collie eye anomaly and a retinal detachment; this eye is unfortunately blind.

GLOSSARY

This glossary is intended to help you, the Griffon Bruxellois owner, better understand the specific terms used in this book as well as other terms that might surface in discussions with your veterinary surgeon during his care of your Griffon Bruxellois.

Abscess a pus-filled inflamed area of body tissue.

Acral lick granuloma unexplained licking of an area, usually the leg, that prevents healing of original wound.

Acute disease a disease whose onset is sudden and fast.

Albino an animal totally lacking in pigment (always white).

Allergy a known sensitivity that results from exposure to a given allergen.

Alopecia lack of hair.

Amaurosis an unexplained blindness from the retina.

Anaemia red-blood-cell deficiency.

Arthritis joint inflammation.

Atopic dermatitis congenital-allergen-caused inflammation of the skin.

Atrophy wasting away caused by faulty nutrition; a reduction in size.

Bloat gastric dilatation.

Calculi mineral 'stone' located in a vital organ, ie, gall bladder.

Cancer a tumour that continues to expand and grow rapidly.

Carcinoma cancerous growth in the skin.

Cardiac arrhythmia irregular heartbeat.

Cardiomyopathy heart condition involving the septum and flow of blood.

Cartilage strong but pliable body tissue.

Cataract clouding of the eye lens.

Cherry eye third eyelid prolapsed gland.

Cleft palate improper growth of the two hard palates of the mouth.

Collie eye anomaly congenital defect of the back of the eye.

Congenital not the same as hereditary, but present at birth.

Congestive heart failure fluid buildup in lungs due to heart's inability to pump.

Conjunctivitis inflammation of the membrane that lines eyelids and eyeball.

Cow hocks poor rear legs that point inward; always incorrect.

Cryptorchid male animal with only one or both testicles undescended.

Cushing's disease condition caused by adrenal gland producing too much corticosteroid.

Cyst uninflamed swelling contain non-pus-like fluid.

Degeneration deterioration of tissue.

Demodectic mange red-mite infestation caused by *Demodex canis*.

Dermatitis skin inflammation.

Dew claw a functionless digit found on the inside of a dog's leg.

Diabetes insipidus disease of the hypothalamus gland resulting in animal passing great amounts of diluted urine.

Diabetes mellitus excess of glucose in blood stream.

Distemper contagious viral disease of dogs that can be most deadly.

Distichiasis double layer of eyelashes on an eyelid.

Dysplasia abnormal, poor development of a body part, especially a joint.

Dystrophy inherited degeneration.

Eclampsia potentially deadly disease in post-partum bitches due to calcium deficiency.

Ectropion outward turning of the eyelid; opposite of entropion.

Eczema inflammatory skin disease, marked by itching.

Edema fluid accumulation in a specific area.

Entropion inward turning of the eyelid.

Epilepsy chronic disease of the nervous system characterized by seizures.

Exocrine pancreatic insufficiency body's inability to produce enough enzymes to aid digestion.

False pregnancy pseudo-pregnancy, bitch shows all signs of pregnancy but there is no fertilization.

Follicular mange demodectic mange.

Gastric dilatation bloat caused by the dog's swallowing air resulting in distended, twisted stomach.

Gastroenteritis stomach or intestinal inflammation.

Gingivitis gum inflammation caused by plaque buildup.

Glaucoma increased eye pressure affecting vision.

Haematemesis vomiting blood.

Haematoma blood-filled swollen area.

Haematuria blood in urine.

Haemophilia bleeding disorder due to lack of clotting factor.

Haemorrhage bleeding.

Heat stroke condition due to over-heating of an animal.

Heritable an inherited condition.

Hot spot moist eczema characterised by dog's licking in same area.

Hyperglycemia excess glucose in blood.

Hypersensitivity allergy.

Hypertrophic cardiomyopathy left-ventricle septum becomes thickened and obstructs blood flow to heart.

Hypertrophic osteodystrophy condition affecting normal bone development.

Hypothyroidism disease caused by insufficient thyroid hormone.

Hypertrophy increased cell size resulting in enlargement of organ.

Hypoglycemia glucose deficiency in blood.

Idiopathic disease of unknown cause.

IgA deficiency immunoglobin deficiency resulting in digestive, breathing and skin problems.

Inbreeding mating two closely related animals, eg, mother—son.

Inflammation the changes that occur to a tissue after injury, characterised by swelling, redness, pain, etc.

Jaundice yellow colouration of mucous membranes.

Keratoconjunctivitis sicca dry eye.

Leukaemia malignant disease charac-terised by white blood cells released into blood stream.

Lick granuloma excessive licking of a wound, preventing proper healing.

Merle coat colour that is diluted.

Monorchid a male animal with only one testicle descended.

Neuritis nerve inflammation.

Nicitating membrane third eyelid pulling across the eye.

Nodular dermatofibrosis lumps on toes and legs, usually associated with cancer of kidney and uterus.

Osteochondritis bone or cartilage inflammation.

Outcrossing mating two breed representatives from different families.

Pancreatitis pancreas inflammation.

Pannus chronic superficial keratitis, affecting pigment and blood vessels of cornea.

Panosteitis inflammation of leg bones, characterised by lameness.

Papilloma wart.

Patellar luxation slipped kneecap, common in small dogs.

Patent ductus arteriosus an open blood vessel between pulmonary artery and aorta.

Penetrance frequency in which a trait shows up in offspring of animals carrying that inheritable trait.

Periodontitis acute or chronic inflam-mation of tissue surround the tooth.

Pneumonia lung inflammation.

Progressive retinal atrophy congenital disease of retina causing blindness.

Pruritis persistent itching.

Retinal atrophy thin retina.

Seborrhea dry scurf or excess oil deposits on the skin.

Stomatitis mouth inflammation.

Tumour solid or fluid-filled swelling resulting from abnormal growth.

Uremia waste product buildup in blood due to disease of kidneys.

Uveitis inflammation of the iris.

Von Willebrand's disease hereditary bleeding disease.

Wall eye lack of colour in the iris.

Weaning separating the mother from her dependent, nursing young.

Zoonosis animal disease communicable to humans.

INDEX

*Page numbers in **boldface** indicate illustrations.*

Adult diet 70
Affenpinscher 9
Age 93
Aggression
—fear 102
Agility trials 111
Alexandra Palace Show 16
Allergy 120
—airborne 126
—food 32
American Journal of Cardiology 27
American Kennel Club 23, 38
Anal glands 82
Ancylostoma caninum 140, **141**
As Good as It Gets 14
Ascaris lumbricoides 139
Australia 21
Axelrod, Dr Herbert R 139
Baigneuse au Griffon, La 23
Barbu 23
Bathing 78
Bedding 48
Boarding 85
Bolton Woods Mixer 10
Bones 51
Bowls 52
Breed name 23
Breed standard 35, 38
Breeder
—finding a 51
Brown dog tick **135**
Bruno 15
Brussels Griffon 23
Canine development schedule 93
Canine parvovirus 122
Canis 15
Cars 83
Cat 100
Cataracts **152**
Champion 9
Chien, Le 23
Cherry eye 150
Chest 26

Chewing 65, 95
Cheyletiella 138
Club du Griffon Bruxellois 10
Coat 27
Collar 52, 101
—selection 53
Collie eye **153**
Colostrum 69
Come 106
Commands 94, 102
Conjunctiva 149
Conjunctivitis 149
Copthorne 11
Copthorne Pasha 16
Copthorne Talk o' the Town 15
Copthorne Top-o'-the-Tree 16
Corneal disease 150
Corneal edema **151**
Coronavirus 115
Crate 47, 49, 63, 83, 94, 96
—training 49, 96
Cropping 20
Crufts Dog Show 15
Crying 63
Ctenocephalides **133**
Ctenocephalides canis **130-131**
Cushing's disease 124
Dangerfield, Stanley 24, 28
de Empolin, Jacope 23
Dental health 129
Dermacentor variabilis **135-136**, 37
Dermatitis 32
Deworming programme 140
Diet 67
—adult 70
—change in 74
—grain-based 69
—puppy 69
—senior 72
Dignity and Impudence 12
Dirofilaria immitis 142
Discipline 99
Distemper 115
Distichiasis 149

Documents 43
Dog flea **130-131**
Dog tick **137**
Down 103
Dry eye syndrome 149
Dutch Smoushond 23
Ear cleaning 82
Ear cropping 20
Earl, Maud 9
Echinococcus multilocularis 141
Ectopic cilia 149
Ectropion 148
Eczema 32
English Toy Spaniel 9
Entropion **148**
Exercise 73
Expression 14
—monkey-like 19
External parasites 130-138
Eye disease 148-153
Eye problems 148
Eyelash abnormalities 149
Fairman, Frances C 12
FCI 38
Fear period 61
Fédération Cynologique Interna-tional 38
Feeding 66
Fence 55
First aid 143
Flea **130-132, 133, 134-135**
—life cycle 131, **134**
Fletcher 14
Food 66, 68
—allergy 32, 127
—intolerance 127
—preference 67
—proper diet 67
—puppy 69
—storage 66
—treats 109
Fox 9
Gender 45
Glaucoma 151, **152**
Good Companions, The 28
Gordon, Miss Adela 14
Griffon 23
Griffon Bruxellois Club 14
Grooming 74
—equipment 76

Head 25
Health
—dental 129
Heartworm **142**
Helene, Princess 15
Heel 107
Hepatitis 115
Homeopathic remedies 32
Hookworm 140, **141**
—larva **140**
Housetraining 91
—schedule 97
Identification 86-87
Internal parasites 139-142
Irish Terrier 9, **10**
Kennel Club, The 15, 35, 38, 43
—breed standard 35, 37
—registration 21
Kennel cough 115, 120
Keratoconjunctivitis sicca **149**
King Charles Spaniel 9, **12**, 19, 31
Kingscote, Mrs 14
Kuhn, Dwight R 135
Ladies Kennel Association Show 14
Landing, Mme 11
Landseer, Sir Edwin 12
Lead 51, 101
Lens dislocation 152
Lens luxation **153**
Leptospirosis 115
Lice 138
Lid conformational abnormalities 148
Lindane 138
Lupus 126
Mange 138
—mite **138**
Marquant Miss Scarlet 22
Marriage of Arnolfini and Giovanna Cenani, The 23
Mary, Queen 19
Milk 70
Mite 135
—infestation 82
Mousequetaire Rouge 15
Nail clipping 80
Navvy's dog 13
Netherlands 23
Neutering 121

New Zealand 21
Nicholson, Jack 14
Nipping 62
Nutrition 73
Obedience class 88, 109
Optic nerve 153
Optic neuritis 153
Parasite
—bites 126
—external 130-138
—internal 139-142
Partridge Hill Kennels 9
Parvovirus 115
Pearch, Mrs Frank 14
Personality 24
Petit Brabançon 18-19
Pollen allergy 126
Prolapse of the gland **149**, 150
Prolapsed gland 149
Psoroptes bovis **138**
Pug **12**, 19
Punishment 100
Puppy
—appearance 42
—family introduction 56
—food 69
—health 120
—home preparation 46
—ownership 42
—problems 60, 62
—selection 43
—socialisation 62
—training 90
Puppy-proofing 54, 57
Pyrame 31
Rabies 115
Ranelagh show 15
Retinal disease 152
Retinal dysplasia **153**
Rhabditis **139**
Rhipicephalus sanguineus **135**
Rhodes, Mrs Parker 9, 11
Rouge 16
Roundworm **139**, 140
Royal Melbourne Show 21
SARD 153
Seasonal Affected Disorder 75
Senior diet 72
Separation anxiety 63
Sit 102

Size 19, 25, 27
Skin problems 32, 123
—inherited 124
Smooth-coat 27
Socialisation 60-61, 63
Spicer, Lady Handley 10-12, 14
Stable E'curie 10
Stay 105
Stockes, Vernon 15
Stripping 75
Sweden 23
Tapeworm 140, **141**
Teeth 82
Thorndike's Theory of Learning 100
Thorndike, Dr Edward 100
Tick 135
Tom 9
Toxocara canis 139
Toys 49-51
Tracheobronchitis 120
Training 61
—consistency 106
—crate 96
—equipment 101
—puppy 90
Travelling
—air 84
—car 83
Treats 101
Tresaderm 138
Turn-up 26
Uncinaria stenocephala 140
USA 23
Urinary tract disease 117
Uveitis 151
Vaccinations 54, 86, 117, 121
van Eyck, Jan 9, 23
Veterinary surgeon 56, 113, 121, 126, 133, 140
Vom 9
Water 70, 73
Web feet 20, 31
Weight 25, 27
Whin 19
Whining 63
Wilson, Mr S 10
World War I 20
World War II 20
Yorkshire Terrier 9, **13**

My Griffon Bruxellois

PUT YOUR PUPPY'S FIRST PICTURE HERE

Dog's Name _____

Date _____ Photographer _____